D1423919

Evolutionary Leadership

DR. DON BECK, COAUTHOR, SPIRAL DYNAMICS:
*"Unlike many who profess to grasp Spiral Dynamics or the Integral
perspective, Peter Merry is breaking the codes of the spiral itself and is
uniquely able to make this knowledge understandable and applicable.
He roams freely between rich conceptual insights and the capacity to
mobilize others to focus on practical problems in our complex and
chaotic worlds. Evolutionary Leadership meshes insights from
cutting-edge research while surfing the froth of transformational
change. This is a must read for those who are struggling to identify
and connect more of the dots."*

PROF. ERVIN LASZLO, PHYSICIST, AUTHOR THE AKASHIC FIELD:
*"We need leadership that moves our world beyond the status quo, for
the status quo is not tenable – the essence of 'unsustainability.' This
means that we need evolutionary leadership. Peter Merry's book gives
the gist of why we need it and, above all, what we can do about it:
how we can become a responsible 'evolutionary leader.' Recommended
reading for everyone seeking to be a responsible, aware, and modest
but true leader."*

HERMAN WIJFFELS, RETIRED, FORMER DUTCH DIRECTOR OF THE WORLD
BANK, CHAIR OF THE DUTCH SOCIAL AND ECONOMIC COUNCIL AND CEO
OF RABOBANK:
*"I find this a wonderful book and recognised a lot in it, as well as
learned a lot from it. It is a great synthesis of what leading thinkers*

such as Wilber, Beck and Cohen have developed over the last years, all with a personal flavour. That in itself would be a worthy publication. But you also identify the consequences of this perspective in what I see as a new way, and take it to a practical level for individuals as well as for organisations. Theory and practice in one, and short and succinct at that. Good work!"

MARIANNE DE JAGER, *IBM NEDERLAND N.V., BUSINESS CONSULTANT, AND* RENÉ VAN DEN BERG, *IBM NEDERLAND N.V., BUSINESS MANAGER BUSINESS CONTINUITY & RECOVERY SERVICES:*
"Practice is the best teacher for what Peter Merry addresses in his book Evolutionary Leadership. *To apply what you unconditionally believe in with great care for all involved is a first step towards sustainable engagement, belief and motivation. In IBM (Netherlands) we are applying Peter Merry's ideas with success. We are creating an environment where mutual trust forms the basis for transformation and within which new insights can be carried and applied in an integral approach. Surprising new forms of co-operation are emerging which create space for everyone's contribution. It takes time but is contributing in all aspects to the satisfaction of employees and clients, and therefore also to increased turnover. And most importantly it brings joy back into the workplace. The experiences that we have had so far with Peter Merry and* Evolutionary Leadership *ask for more."*

PABLO SMOLDERS, *DIRECTOR, DUTCH:*
"Peter has captured the spirit of everybody's everyday actions on humankind's future development. Evolutionary Leadership *is a very inspirational book which addresses both theory & practice from a variety of angles. Peter travels from collective consciousness to individual responsibility, from ancient roots to future generations and from emotional intuition to rational roadmaps. He never fades into*

softness nor teaching while facilitating our road to consciousness.
"Peter writes easy-to-get and sketches with poetic reflections. He is able to get a message across which will be adopted by our generation already realising that well-being originates in self-reflection and transcends the ordinary western well-fare well. Peter simply directs & guides us toward the logical consequences and takes us all the way down to the final step: the leader within ourselves.

"Peter has inspired me to even go further in striving to incorporate future well-being goals into my daily life. I do strongly recommended this book not only to my own staff & clients but to everybody who is searching for wholeness & unity and the inspiration to truly find inner peace. I only can hope that leadership in political, business and scientific domain will further support this movement and Peter will keep up the good work with the Center for Human Emergence.

"Peter clearly has touched upon and tapped into his own passion to lead, who dares to follow? Who said complexity can not be simplified?"

JOHN BUNZL, FOUNDER, INTERNATIONAL SIMULTANEOUS POLICY ORGANISATION:
"Evolutionary Leadership is the essential guide to wholeness – in society, in business, in the world and in our deepest selves. Combining the latest in integral thinking and drawing on key change techniques and practices including Open Space, Chaordic Design and Collective Intelligence, Merry points the way towards the vital and urgent evolutionary transformation of ourselves, our organisations and our world."

NICK WILDING, CHAIR, CENTRE FOR HUMAN ECOLOGY, SCOTLAND:
"Engage! have rapidly proven themselves to be experiential learning innovators of the first order. It is no wonder they are highly sought after as consultants in organisational evolution. That's why I was so keen to learn the secrets of what makes them so effective first hand. I

wasn't disappointed. With Evolutionary Leadership, Peter Merry has broken new ground again – this is the first book I have read that convincingly shares practical, visionary thinking with a rapidly growing wider community of 'integral' facilitation practice. And what a treasure trove of innovation! This is a sourcebook that has challenged me to deepen my own engagement with integral spiral dynamics theory, and has convinced me that evolutionary thinking and practice are of critical importance if humankind is to face the complex challenges of global ecological sustainability and social justice."

RORY HENDRIKS, *ASHRIDGE INTERNATIONAL BUSINESS SCHOOL:*
"I was left feeling full of admiration and even hopeful about our future possibilities of reconnecting people to our world. The writing style is both both insightful and accessible, it has a genuine quality about it – refreshing in our largely egocentric world."

MARLENE DE BEER, *SOUTH AFRICAN BORN SCHOLAR-POET; MA SOC.SC.; PHD CANDIDATE, UNESCO CENTRE, UNIVERSITY OF ULSTER:*
"Peter Merry's Evolutionary Leadership *is written in an essay reading and flowing manner that may conceal to some readers the great depth of reflection from which it originates. I not only recommend this book to anyone who is new to Beck's Spiral Dynamics integral and Wilber's 4 Quadrants, but also to those who are familiar with these and related authors. All will be inspired and refreshed by how Peter applies these theories and models to* Evolutionary Leadership *that are so crucial for our times... Peter invites you into a tetra-evolutionary spiral dance to explore new shores. The time is now – flow in!"*

Peter Merry

Evolutionary Leadership

INTERGRAL LEADERSHIP FOR AN INCREASINGLY COMPLEX WORLD

Integral Publishers

English Version
Published by Integral Publishers
http://www.integralleadershipreview.com
733 Mermaid Avenue
Pacific Grove, California, USA 93950
831 333-9200
1. Business 2. Management Science
For more information about Integral Publishers
russ@integralleadershipreview.com
Integral Publishers, 733 Mermaid Avenue
Pacific Grove, CA 93950
(831) 333-9200

ISBN-13: 978-0-615-26904-7
ISBN-10: 0-615-26904-7

Dutch Version

Graphic Design by Wim ten Brinke BNO, wtbrinke@qnet.nl

Dedication

For the good of the whole

Gratitude

Many of those whose vision, ideas and practice have inspired this book are already named later on. I would like to pick out a couple who have played a particularly significant role. Dr Don Beck, founder of Spiral Dynamics Integral and the Center for Human Emergence, has supported me strongly since we first met in Germany in 2001. His passion for action for the good of the whole is extremely infectious. I am also continually in awe of the effort that Ken Wilber makes to see how every theory and practice that exists contributes to the whole, regardless of what people think about it. Although we have never met, his incessant quest for truth and email encouragement for the path I am on lifts my spirit continually. I also have Andrew Cohen to thank for his courage in standing up and speaking out what is not always a popular message. He has certainly given my ego plenty to chew on, and it is largely thanks to his teachings that I am learning to make myself more available to the evolutionary impulse flowing through me.

Herman Wijffels has been of great support to me in manifesting this in my current place of residence, the Netherlands. Simply on the basis of a couple of meetings and this book, he has shown the kind of faith in me that encourages me to step out into the world with more confidence and with the knowledge that I have something of significance to offer. It will prove to have been an important meeting. Flowing from that, I'd like to thank Chris van Gelderen at Altamira-Becht for his faith and his rapidity of action in getting this book out first in Dutch when it became clear that there was a call for it. For the English edition, Helen Titchen Beeth has been of great support stubbornly reminding me that I should be doing more to get it out there, and Russ Volckmann was the right man in the right place with the right heart to take the plunge and actually publish it. Thank you so much.

I'd also like to thank all those people who have been part of our adventure at the Center for Human Emergence (Netherlands) for the learning journey we are on, and for showing the kind of faith and commitment in this journey which emergence will find very hard to resist.

This book would not have come to fruition without the unflinching support of my initial business partners at Engage! InterAct, Arjen Bos and Tim Merry. As I boldly announced that I was dropping much of my certain old work to make space for the new which wasn't there yet, they stepped into that space of trust with me and supported me for a good six months as I sat with my own process of emergence. After Tim moved to Canada, Tatiana Glad joined us. One of the first things she said was how strongly she resonated with so much of what was in this book. We are now all stepping into making it happen in the world, and I feel immensely supported by Engage! as we move into the unknown.

Finally, my greatest learning over the last years has been in the space of my relationship with my wife Marcella and our two young boys Finnlo and Senne. There's no hiding from oneself in a life partnership. Mirrors all around… If I ever doubted the power of spirit and the evolving Universe, I only need look at the boys to know that great things are at work. I love them all dearly and thank them for being who they are and for choosing me this time round. Thanks then also to my parents for being there for me. On we go…

Contents

Foreword

The world is at one of those key moments in history where it could go either way – break through to a more highly evolved way of living together, or break down into conflict between the diverse social and environmental pressures we are feeling today. How we respond to the situation now will determine the future tomorrow.

Evolutionary Leadership provides a clear map of the landscape that we are currently navigating, a helicopter view of the dynamics of individual and collective development. Given the new realities we are facing, our old maps are proving inadequate. We need new maps to help us see more clearly so we may act more effectively for the good of the whole.

Taking the latest cutting-edge thinking and practice, Peter Merry transforms the complexity into a clear and compelling overview of how it all hangs together, what the implications are for our own personal leadership, and how we might start harnessing the best emerging transformative practices to move humanity forward in the right direction. The power of this book lies in its clarity, passion and immediate applicability.

In my work helping organizations from across the world navigate the creative tensions between powerful extremes of value dilemmas, I encounter daily the complexity that our world is now challenging us with. I know from experience that trying to solve our new problems with the same way of thinking that created them simply will not work (to paraphrase Albert Einstein).

At the same time, these insights tell us that many leaders in the world are poised on the edge of what Clare Graves (the researcher behind Spiral Dynamics) calls "a great leap for humankind". Some argue we can't yet bridge from the old to the new because the stress has not been great enough. Furthermore we have been educated to engage the world in linear ways and find it difficult to deal with dilemmas effectively. We could get them out of the way by simply taking sides. Others, however, tell us we are ready for this leap. And the group of those who do so is gathering momentum. The author of this book is among them. We can either choose to deny this reality and pretend it is not happening, or we can stand up to claim the destiny that is our birthright. It is up to us.

This book provides us with a map and some proven tools. It gives us insight into what an adequate response to these new challenges might look like. Departing from linear thinking, Peter Merry asks us not to take sides, but to integrate opposing values and views, resulting in greater integrity. However, this is not a blueprint which you simply go out and apply. If we take these insights seriously, then we must also get serious about our own personal development. So read this book and be prepared to take responsibility. It is no joke that the last section in the book is called "The Beginning".

FONS TROMPENAARS, *FOUNDER OF TROMPENAARS HAMPDEN-TURNER CONSULTING AND (CO-)AUTHOR OF BEST-SELLING BOOKS* RIDING THE WAVES OF CULTURE *AND* SERVANT LEADERSHIP ACROSS CULTURES. *WISDOM COUNCIL MEMBER, CENTER FOR HUMAN EMERGENCE, NETHERLANDS*

Introduction

Time to Awaken

Hello, this is 'Time to Awaken'
The new James Bond:
I want you stirred and shaken.
Can you feel the quickenin'?
Can you feel the flickerin'?
Deep down in the belly
Turn off the telly
Sorry if you was havin' a nap
Listen up to what I rap
It's worth the hear
Break it down to what's becoming clear ...

Here we go:
We all be learners and teachers
We don't need no preachers
To find the whole
soul
force
Of course!
It is like riding a horse
remaining in the saddle
even when up shit creek without a paddle.

Be yourself
Everyone else is taken
No point fakin

The only person you're foolin' is yourself
You already got all the wealth
Don't need to search no more
Knocking door to door
Cause its all in the place you was born in
No more stallin'
Listen loudly to the callin'
Why you here?
It ain't nothing to do with fear
That much is clear.

I must confess
my greatest fear was success
Daring to shine bright
Get into the line of sight
Stepping into the spotlight.
I trained for years
To be on stage and hide my fears
In the character of another
Always under cover
Never truly the deeper me
Time to see
Be free
Be

Now
Fear no more
I am sure
I have felt the
Whole
Soul Force
Course
Through my veins

I know what it means to be sane
Living in partnership with my brain
My body and blood
And the un-nameable flood
Of realisation
Be Self
Everyone else is taken
It is time to awaken.
Are you stirred and shakin'?
Are you quakin'?
If not why not?
Take a look around
The world is calling to become profound
The message's loud and clear
Drop the fear
The time is now
The place is here.
It's always the occasion
Don't get lost in the alien invasion
Take action
to let go of distraction
Feel the heart
In the breath of the now
Kaboom kapow
Like a hit on head
Sit up in bed
The nightmare is over
You just found the four leaf clover
Ego move over
I am getting on my horse
The whole Soul
force of course!

No more fakin'
be Self
everyone else is taken

It's time to
Awaken

(BY TIM MERRY)

So. Here we are. The unfolding edge of the universe. Welcome.

So what now?

I have written this book because it feels like what is needed right now. It also feels like something I have to offer to the emerging whole at this moment in time. It is written for people who are feeling the edge we are on, who sense that something is inadequate about the way in which we *homo sapiens sapiens* are generally organising ourselves, and who are looking to make sense of things again, to find a role for themselves in this context. There can be no doubt that we are in a period of significant transition. It is tough to live in the old system while the new one is emerging. This book is my contribution to the emergence of the new.

We find ourselves at a particularly significant juncture in our collective development. We feel emotionally and know intellectually the great stress that our planet and our civilisation are under. We also sense in some way the great opportunity that lies before us. What reaches my ears is that we have a limited number of years to embrace that opportunity or be part of the next Great Extinction.

The official systems term for this situation we find ourselves in is a "bifurcation" point, literally: a place where the road forks in two. One of the ways leads to breakthrough and transcendence, the other to breakdown and regression. As ever, it is our choice which one we take.

What has brought us to this point? Our solutions to a previous set of challenges. The solutions to one set of problems sow the seeds for the next set of problems, and therefore for the next solutions. And on it goes – forever, as far as we know.

The particular challenge we are now facing is one of separation. In our excitement and enthusiasm for the powers of discovery that we have developed in ourselves, we have become too detached from the very context we live in. The systems and structures that we have created around us now reflect that sense of separation, embedding us in a context that is hard to break out of. "I" has become separate from "You", "Them" and "It".

What we are witnessing is the natural dance of yang and yin – of assertion and connection. We are currently far along in the swing to the assertion side. If we are open enough to the feedback from around us, calling us forward to a new form of connection, and if we are able to adapt quickly enough, we will survive to dance onwards and upwards. If we fail to respond in time, the tension will become too great and we will be pulled back, kicking and screaming. Our progress will be checked. This is the natural order.

We are currently stretching our distance from the yin energy of connectedness to a critical point. We are nearing the limit, and the window of opportunity in which we can make a conscious choice to reconnect and evolve onwards is narrowing. If we miss the chance, we are on course to be brought back to earth, literally, with a vicious bump. Then we'll know what connectedness is all about!

So the need is to find new connection, to feel and understand the context we are part of. This is not about a romanticised "going back to nature", but about aligning ourselves with all that we have discovered in recent times about the nature of life.

As we inquire into the nature of life, from both our own interior experience and our exterior exploration, we discover that the world we are a part of is evolving. It is not evolving randomly, but has a general directionality. The longer-term perspective shows us moving towards greater complexity and greater compassion. That doesn't mean that there won't be many regressions along the way. It means that the spirit of evolution moves in that general direction, looking for forms to express its urge towards increasing wholeness. We are part of that co-creation.

So as we look to reconnect, the world we find ourselves part of is an evolving one. In order to reconnect to our world, therefore, we need to connect to evolution. Looking at what we know about evolution, we can see some general trends in how it works, some patterns of behaviour. Connecting to evolution involves aligning ourselves with those trends.

This book, both in its form and its content, is an attempt to do just that. By touching on a number of different maps all pointing to this landscape, my intention is to direct our attention to the underlying patterns, to get a deeper sense of the landscape itself. I do not attempt to give a comprehensive description of the different maps and models – you can get those from the original sources. Rather, I wish to highlight the essence of each of the maps, and the deeper field that the different perspectives are pointing to. Below, I outline some of the core trends we have become aware of, and show how they are reflected in the structure of the book.

Express-self	Sacrifice-self
Yang	Yin
Agency	Communion
Doing	Being
Transcend	Include
Diversity generation	Conformity enforcement
Risk	Insurance
I	We
Wholeness	Partness
Masculine	Feminine

TABLE 1-1: *Yin-Yan Dynamic*

One core trend that I have already referred to above is the dance between yin and yang, and how that dance triggers evolution and development. Another way of understanding and feeling this dance is to see it as a dance between whole-ness and part-ness, between my identity as a unique whole and my belonging to bigger contexts. If I over-emphasise my individual identity, I begin to feel lonely. If I over-emphasise my belonging, I begin to lose my sense of who I am. The dance is about how we fit within our contexts – our "fit-ness". The following table shows other expressions of this essential dynamic.

Throughout the book, I will come back to this essential dynamic, using the yin-yang language in the sense described above. If the words "yin" and "yang" are not meaningful for

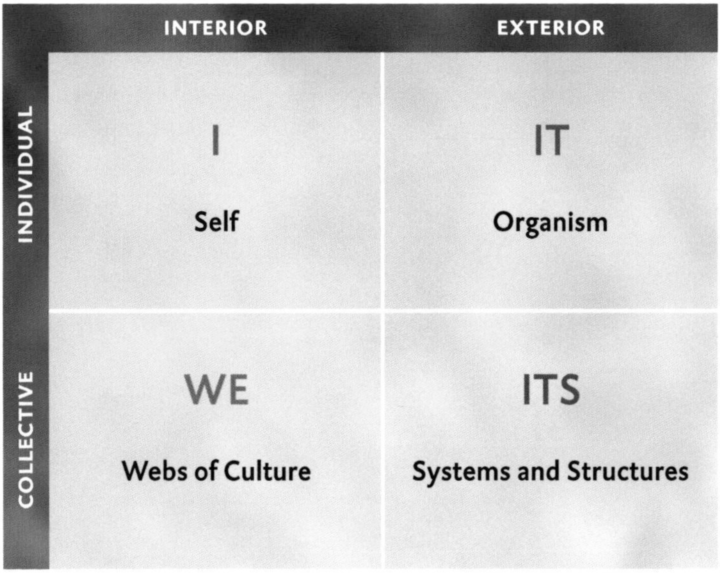

	INTERIOR	EXTERIOR
INDIVIDUAL	**I** Self	**IT** Organism
COLLECTIVE	**WE** Webs of Culture	**ITS** Systems and Structures

FIGURE I-1: *The Four Quadrants; From Wilber (2000)*

you, feel free to replace those words in your mind with any of the pairs in the table above, or your own equivalent. I am also aware that this may not be the way the terms were intended for use by their originators (although it may well be too). However, they speak to me in this way, and the classic yin-yang image beautifully captures the sense of the dynamic dance, so this is how I am using them. What is important is that you feel the essence beyond the words.

Ken Wilber has developed a framework that illustrates this context with great clarity. It has been a useful tool for me over recent years, and I have used it to structure this book. We can notice that whatever phenomenon we choose to look at, these four quadrants are always at play. The two columns represent interior and exterior, and the two rows represent individual and collective.

We can notice that whatever phenomenon we choose to look at, these four quadrants are always at play. The two columns represent interior and exterior, and the two rows represent individual and collective.

The interior is the invisible: what goes on inside an individual and between individuals, in terms of belief systems, values and morals. We cannot scientifically measure this. We have to talk to people in order to discover it.

The exterior is what we can see and measure. It is for example the brain, as opposed to the mind on the interior. We can put sensors on the brain to measure what happens to it when people go into meditative states. This gives us lots of data about the functioning of the brain, but tells us nothing about the person's experience of mind while in that state.

The individual interior is therefore about our personal inner state. This includes for example emotions, cognition, interpersonal capacity and awareness. It is about how we experience the world as it arises around us.

The individual exterior is about our physical organism – including our brain, our nervous system, our muscles, our organs and our behaviour.

The collective interior is about the space that we create between ourselves as we interact: the collective meaning, collective values and expectations about the way we will be together.

The collective exterior is about the systems and structures that we create around us. This can be everything from the way we structure our meetings, to the way we organise ourselves internationally to deal with global challenges, including for example architecture, urban planning, education and health systems and governance systems.

Evolution is about the interaction between all four quadrants – what Wilber calls "tetra-evolution" ("tetra" meaning four). All four quadrants are continually interacting with each other in a spiral dance. There is continual interplay between how I make sense of my world, the people around me, the systems I interact with and the development of my physical organism.

Aligning ourselves with evolution therefore means taking all four of these quadrants into account, in our analyses and understandings, as well as in our action. This is a core part of any integral evolutionary perspective, and the basis of the book.

I have structured this book in seven main sections. Chapter 1 looks at the universal evolutionary tendencies that apply to each of the quadrants and their interaction. Chapter 2 looks in more detail at the situation we find ourselves in now on planet Earth. The next four sections take each quadrant in turn and explore what it means to lead from an evolutionary perspective in that quadrant. So, what is the inner experience of connecting to this perspective, and how can I develop the inner qualities needed to act from it (Chapter 3)? How can I consciously nurture my body to support me in this work (Chapter 4)? What does it feel like to be in a relationship with others from this perspective (Chapter 5)? What systems and structures could support our being together in this way, and what are some of the tools we can use to facilitate their emergence (Chapter 6)?

Finally, Chapter 7 explores how we might get started as we engage the world.

You can read the book in different ways. From cover to cover follows the flow that I wrote it in, so all the references to earlier chapters will make sense. However, if you are not such a fan of the mental maps and understandings offered in the first two chapters, you might like to jump to Chapters 3 and 5, which are more about the inner experience. Chapter 6 contains many examples of tools and processes you can use in organisations. You may be tempted to skip straight to this chapter, but I would encourage you to explore at least some of the earlier chapters first to get a sense of the context. Whatever you choose to do, remember that it is important that we develop *both* our insight *and* our compassion. So if you generally prefer the cognitive realm, experiment with opening up to Chapters 3 and 5. If, on the other hand, you are tempted to run straight to the inner experience, allow yourself space to engage with the mental models. We need both. It's good training for evolutionary leadership.

Throughout the book, I have included little stories from my experience to illustrate the point being made. I draw primarily on two cases. One is that of a leader I have been supporting over recent years who leads a business unit in a multinational technology corporation. The other is that of my own experience of leading the Center for Human Emergence in the Netherlands. Occasionally I also introduce other one-off stories.

At the start of each chapter, you will also find poems written by my brother Tim Merry. He calls it "conscious slam". Each poem is designed to link to the theme of the section it is in. The best way to read them is out loud. On the website (www.kongska.com), you can find links to the poems set to music. In addition to Tim's contribution, George Pór kindly wrote the section on Communities of Practice in Chapter 6.

Once again, I invite you not to allow yourself to be disturbed if you find yourself feeling that the descriptions of some of the models and maps are incomplete. They are bound to be – each one has its own book or books! Rather than trying to grasp the intricate details of each perspective, I invite you to settle back, relax and allow the deeper patterns to arise in your consciousness. I will provide all the references you need to satiate your hunger to know about any of the different maps, models, authors and practices mentioned. See this book as an entry point into a whole new world. It is only a beginning.

Given that the universe is emerging right now in every consecutive moment, it seemed to me that if I was going to be as congruent as possible with the way the universe works, then I should also write this book in an emergent way. When I have written in the past, I have tried to create different sections by clustering notes on cards, relating them to each other and then working out what order they should come in. This time, after connecting through meditation every morning, I started writing and trusted that what emerged would be the right thing. It was remarkable how easily it all flowed. Normally I was writing about one thousand words per hour, which fellow book-writers tell me is a lot. It certainly didn't feel rushed, and everything that I thought needed to be in here found a place somewhere. And it didn't end up too long!

I have also added a bibliography of the books that have inspired me on my way to writing this book. I have generally avoided quoting people directly, as this didn't fit with the emergent writing style. There are also many web resources to support us in developing evolutionary leadership. Because the internet evolves so quickly, I have generally not listed websites, but provide up-to-date links on the website www.evolutionary-leadership.com.

Evolutionary leadership is about leading from an integral evolutionary perspective. My understanding of "integral evolutionary" is described in detail below. Leadership is about taking responsibility for acting on and from that perspective.

This book crystallised after a time of deep reflection and sense making. Once I had clarity again, all the signs told me I should write. Margaret Wheatley once said to me that she knows she is on the right path when the synchronicity is strong. It has been very strong for this book. I trust it finds you at the right time.

I am the universe writing about itself. You are the universe reading about itself.

CHAPTER ONE

How It All Hangs Together

Pushing

My growing and letting go
Not for the show
No
Not alone
We were pushing together
Despite the heavy weather
Expanding heart and mind
Becoming kind
Searching to find
A path in these crazy times
Align all the signs
As I feel my friendships bind
Lift me above the confusion
The illusion
That I gotta have it under control
When really, all I gotta do is roll
With the shifting seas
Bend my knees
Gather community
Round me
Learning to see
This is world of plenty
There's always enough
Even when the going gets tough
Always enough

Just enough
When the seas get rough
My friends and lovers and fellow rovers
You are all my four leaf clovers

Here's to
Pushing
Expanding
Evolving
Dissolving

My friends and lovers and fellow rovers
You are all my four leaf clovers
There's always enough
Even when the going gets tough
Always enough
Just enough
When the seas get rough

(BY TIM MERRY)

As we look at ourselves and the world around us, we see certain patterns in the way everything relates to everything else. The exciting thing is that we are not simply all inter-connected in a static web of relationships, but rather we are all spiralling onwards as the expanding universe. Change is the only constant as the spirit of evolution surges through our veins and gives life to the world.

Ever since the big bang 13.7 billion years ago (which is as far back as we can currently trace our history), the universe has been evolving, developing increasingly complex forms as it goes. It has been a journey of continual experimentation, trying out different forms of organising in a search to transcend and include the past in innovative ways. Creation at work. Some experiments work better than others. The whole system learns. Those forms that succeed best in the search for greater complexity and compassion are the ones that perpetuate. Those that prove inadequate to the task, whose experimentation does not add value to the whole, fade away over time as the universe directs resources to the success stories.

Success in this case is not about who can stand out the most above all others, but rather about who or what can best surf the evolutionary wave. Who can best lead a balanced dance between individual creativity and innovation on the one hand, and compassion and responsibility to the whole on the other? What form can best learn from and respond to the world around it, meeting its own needs more effectively and helping others around it to meet theirs? How do we create enough order to hold it all together, whilst opening up to enough chaos to keep us evolving? There is of course no final equation – it is a perpetual dance, the dance of life.

Having some visual images of this journey can help us to see what is happening more clearly.

The Change Cycle

Dr Ichak Adizes' Life Cycle of Systems is a good place to start[*]. It shows us the general progress of a system, be it a value system inside us or an organisation we create. Adizes originally created the Life Cycle for his work with organisations, but the principle remains the same for all quadrants.

There is a period of growth where the system develops in response to a need that it feels around it. This might be an emergent value system that helps us to cope with the world we are perceiving, or an organisation that we create to fulfil a need we see emerging in the market place or in the social sector. Either way, it emerges in interaction with stimuli around it. It requires some work and investment to start with, to stabilise the system and get it going. If that succeeds, then the system takes off and does what it is designed to do, until it reaches its prime (assuming it successfully negotiates other pitfalls along the way, which are dealt with in detail in Adizes' full model). At that point, it has done a good job at meeting the need that it initially emerged to meet, which is why it is performing so successfully. However, now there is energy to spare to look beyond the current horizons and see a wider world. Once glimpsed, we begin to get a sense that the current system is not adequate to meet the need that we are sensing on the horizon. That is a key moment.

---

[*] See *People Referenced* section for more on Ichak Adizes.

At this moment of transition, there are two options. Either we can begin to open up to what we are perceiving, allow it in to disturb our current way of doing things and explore what it has to teach us. Or we can try and deny its existence and bury ourselves in the old, stable, seemingly safe way of doing things. Although the latter option may seem the less threatening in the short-term, denying the emerging world around us and refusing to adapt will only create increasing stress in the longer run. We disconnect ourselves from our context, and the fit between ourselves and the world around us begins to disintegrate. Our fitness disappears – quite literally on the physical level. When we can no longer make sense of the world around us, when we can't find our place in it, we get sick. Organisations* get sick when they hold on to old ways of doing things in the face of a changing world.

Adizes' Life Cycle (Figure 1.1) shows what happens when a system does not adapt: the slow, painful road to death, with the system turning in on itself, internal strife and a lack of engagement and performance in the outside world. It heralds the end of an organisation, and often severe illness for an individual.

What we should be aiming for, then, as evolutionary living systems, is to facilitate the emergence of a new system by listening to the feedback from the world around us, and from our own

---

* Throughout this book I use the term "organisation" in its widest possible sense – to mean "ways in which we organise ourselves", be that a corporation or civil society organisation (which we might more traditionally call organisations), or the global system of cooperation that we are part of. More specific uses of the word will be apparent from the context.

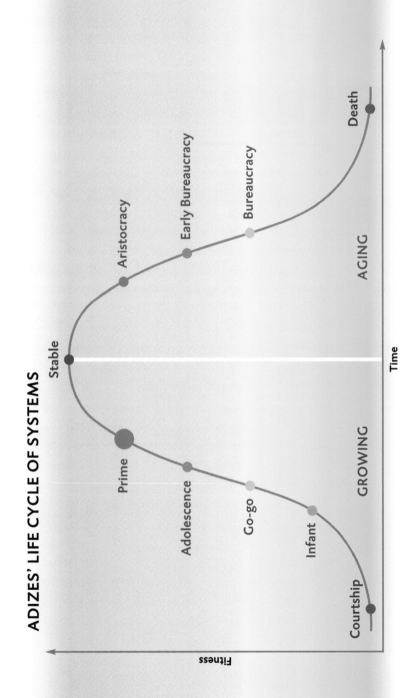

FIGURE 1.1: *Adizes Life Cycle of Systems*

inner voices, and by experimenting with ways to adapt. It is important just to note at this point that holding onto our own essence of who we are is a key part of this process. Adaptation does not mean totally surrendering our individual identity or uniqueness. Rather, if it works well, adaptation actually results in its enhancement. More on this later. Emergence could be depicted as Figure 1.2*.

As the old system reaches its peak, some parts of it sense a need to change. They are sensing a world out there for which the current system is not adequate. Dissonance creeps into the status quo, and insight begins to emerge about how things could be seen and done differently. The parts of the system which sense this are what Howard Bloom (2000) calls Diversity Generators, in his description of five key qualities of a healthy living system**. They are the complement to the Conformity Enforcers who maintain stability, and who will be needed again to stabilise the new system once it comes online. Diversity Generators are stimulated and particularly needed in times of major transition, but given that change is the only constant, they always have some role to play. It is never only one or the other – it is a question of emphasis. Once more, it's all in the dance.

A third property of the evolutionary dance is what Bloom calls Resource Shifting, the capacity to shift energy and stimuli to the

---

* I was introduced to the s-curve concept by Dieuwke Begemann and much of my initial insight around this model emerged in conversations with her. Others have since pointed out to me that the concept has actually been around a very long time, and to assign its origination to any individual would be inappropriate. As ever, it's an impersonal phenomenon.

** See *People Referenced* for more on Howard Bloom.

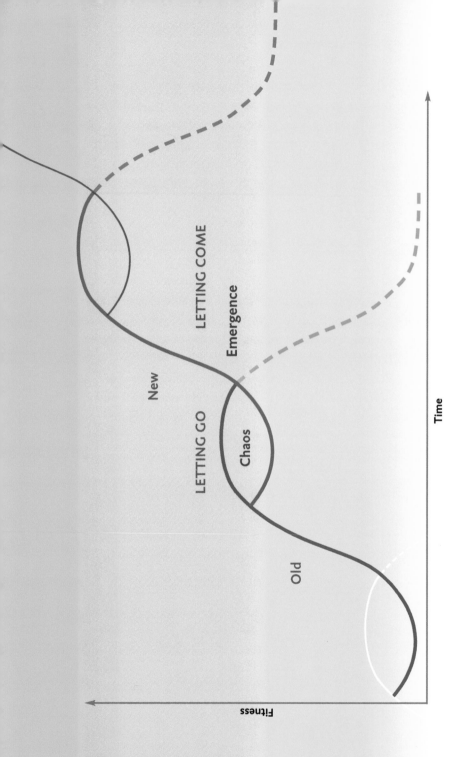

FIGURE 1.2: *Emergence Cycles*

parts of the system that are most needed at that time. So the resources will be channelled to the Diversity Generators when more creativity is needed, and to the Conformity Enforcers when more stability is needed. Resources will also shift to those parts of the system that are most successful at either of those tasks.

In us as individuals, diversity generation happens through our senses, which pick up stimuli from the world around us. We often feel the tension they create in our bodies. Learning to listen to our bodies is a good way of tuning into that feedback.

In organisations, the diversity generators are the change agents. In a negative sense they may be seen as troublemakers, as they continually refer to the problem with the current way of doing things and emphasise the need to change. If they are not listened to, they will usually leave or get sick, as it is too stressful to work in an environment which is not congruent with the world one is experiencing. In a learning organisation which is open to change, their insight will be valued highly – it is the future of the organisation. You will find more on how to work with change agents in Chapter 6.

Story

At the Corporation...I sit waiting at a table in a café at Amsterdam Schiphol airport for a man a friend introduced me to. They both work at the same Corporation. She thought he might be ready to step into leading change. We recognise each other even though we've never met before – funny how that works, isn't it? We shake hands, he sits down, and starts to tell me his story. A story of a journey in the Corporation, from high times of success and fulfilment, to more recent disillusionment and shock at the deteriorating state of the organisation.

He is clearly moved by the suffering of the people in the organisation, and torn between his deep loyalty to the Corporation and anger at how it is treating its people. He told me that he wanted to try to change things, but that if it didn't work, he was ready to leave. Here indeed was a potential change agent, moved deeply and unattached to being rewarded by the system for any change efforts he should make. He was sensing the breakdown of the old, and feeling deep in his soul the potential for the new – even though he had no idea what that might look like.

I listen. Once he is finished, I pull out a pen and sketch Wilber's four quadrants on the back of a paper napkin, suggesting that there is a misfit between his values and desired behaviour, and the culture and structure of the organisation. He enthusiastically affirms that, and says that many more people he has spoken to are experiencing that. The simple fact of seeing a model that explains what is happening releases energy. We analyse a bit more, and agree to take a next step. I suggest the formation of a change community. He likes the idea and will see what he can do to make it happen.

This is to be the start of a long and deep journey together, in which this man initiates a movement of change communities and becomes head of a business unit which we work on transforming. I feel at the end of that first meeting that something of significance is emerging.

In the S-curve graphic in Figure 1-2 we can see that the new, emergent system co-exists for a while with the old organisation before it takes over from it. This is usually a stressful time for all involved in the change, as the diversity generators are having to survive in an old system until the transition happens. It all depends on how open the old system is to change, and how well the emerging new system is supported and nurtured.

This phase is often referred to as the chaos phase, because that is how it feels as the old system breaks down and the new is still emerging. However, Ervin Laszlo (2001) prefers to call it the "Critical Phase", because chaos is often understood as meaning a lack of order. This phase is not about a lack of order, rather it is a place of more subtle order, where small stimuli have an amplified impact. Those stimuli can either pull us towards breakdown or provide energy for breakthrough. Clearly it makes for a delicate time, where it is all the more important to be conscious of the likely impact of our action on the whole.

The S-curve is an evolutionary pattern that has been identified by people from different specialisations. Below, for example, we can see Clare Graves' graphic of psychological development, and Ray Kurzweil's depictions of different areas of technological development – note the mini S-curves within the larger S-curve (courtesy of Ray Kurzweil and KurzweilAI.net), *Figure 1.4-6.*

Note that these patterns become evident in Kurzweil's graphics when they are mapped onto an exponential scale. The rate of change in the universe is increasing exponentially.

When we combine the S-curve with the underlying patterns in the Adizes' life cycle and the Spiral Dynamics stages (Figure 1.7; see Chapter 2 for more on the specifics), we can identify more detailed steps that a system goes through on the S-curve from its interior perspective.

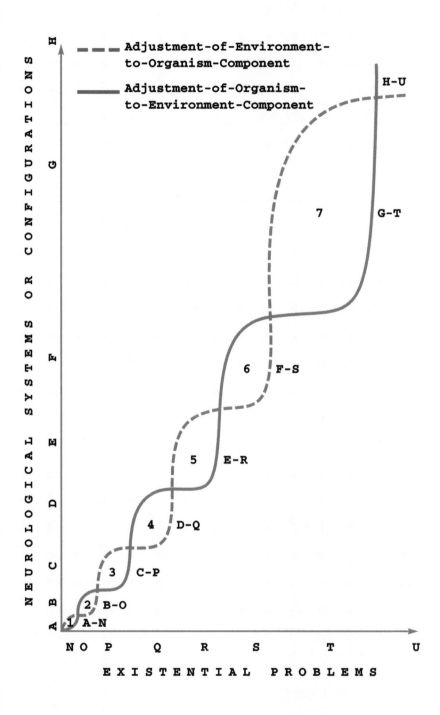

FIGURE 1.3: *Clare Graves' Levels of Human Existence.*

These stages repeat themselves in every new system and S-curve. There is a general pattern to each stage that remains the same, but the way that deeper pattern manifests is different in each system. The colours I have chosen to use reflect the colours of the chakra system, as there seems to be a close connection. Each stage has an evolutionary role.

As the old system begins to lose fitness and a new system begins to form, that new system is driven by a survival need. It is just becoming aware of its own birth and existence. It senses that it exists in an unsupportive environment (the old dominant system) and spends all its energy on maintaining its survival. It has to fight for its own space. As that struggle evolves, people gather around the emerging system and a spirit of belonging emerges. People need to feel that they have companions in this daring adventure, that they have a bigger family and home. Group symbols and rituals help to reinforce that sense of belonging.

As the new system emerges onto the radar screen, it has a need for clear identity. It needs to let others know that it exists, and to be clear about what it stands for in order to establish itself. Once established and recognised, it begins to see itself as part of a bigger context. A whole new world, mythology and belief system emerge within which the new system can make sense of its existence. With its cosmology in place, it turns outwards to manifest new possibilities. This is its most productive phase (what Adizes calls its "prime"). Our identity is clear, our context is clear and the world is our oyster. Out we go out to make our fortune.

However, this adventure out into the world exposes us to an even wider perspective. After a time of playing our role in the world as we thought it was, we begin to get insight into a new world on the horizon. And if we are an open living system, the

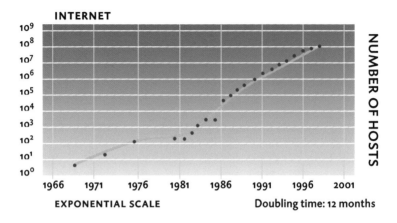

INTERNET

NUMBER OF HOSTS

EXPONENTIAL SCALE   Doubling time: 12 months

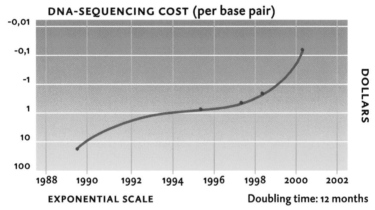

DNA-SEQUENCING COST (per base pair)

DOLLARS

EXPONENTIAL SCALE   Doubling time: 12 months

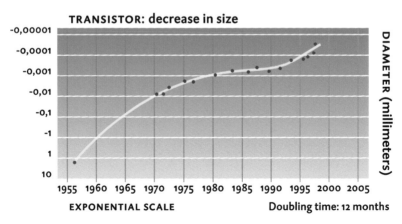

TRANSISTOR: decrease in size

DIAMETER (millimeters)

EXPONENTIAL SCALE   Doubling time: 12 months

FIGURE 1.4-6: *Kurzweil Graphics. Used with permission.*

whole cycle starts again. Otherwise our system will start to go into decline. The decline is an unhealthy version of the healthy ascent (Figure 1.8).

Instead of insight into the new, we get blindness to the new. Instead of manifesting new possibilities, we repeat the old ways. Instead of a fresh, larger context, we get a rigidifying of the old truth. Instead of clarifying a new identity, we hold on to a static old identity. Instead of creating new rituals to express a new sense of belonging, we enforce outdated rituals that suffocate people and spirit. Instead of survival, we get death. When a system enters into decline like this, it suffocates the people who are part of it, draining them of energy in its attempt to hang on to an old way of life. It also creates turbulence and stress in the world around it, as it insists on being a rock in a flowing river. Eventually it will get worn down.

Another way of looking at this process is through the Change State Indicator (Figure 1.9) described by Don Beck and Christopher Cowan (1996). Notice that the vertical axis is "perceived fit with life conditions". The relative place on this axis shows to what extent we are able to make sense of the world around us. An "alpha" fit is where we are fully in tune with the world as we perceive it. As an individual, our internal coping mechanisms are functioning well, and as an organisation or society we are meeting a real need. After a while, having met the current need, our world moves on and our perspective broadens. New challenges begin to appear on our radar screen, which our current system cannot yet resolve. The Beta stage emerges as our fitness is stretched and stress increases. At that point we may be open and responsive enough to adapt to the incoming feedback, and Flex up to the next Alpha fit. Or we may fail to learn and adapt and, as the stress builds, the barriers loom until we crash down

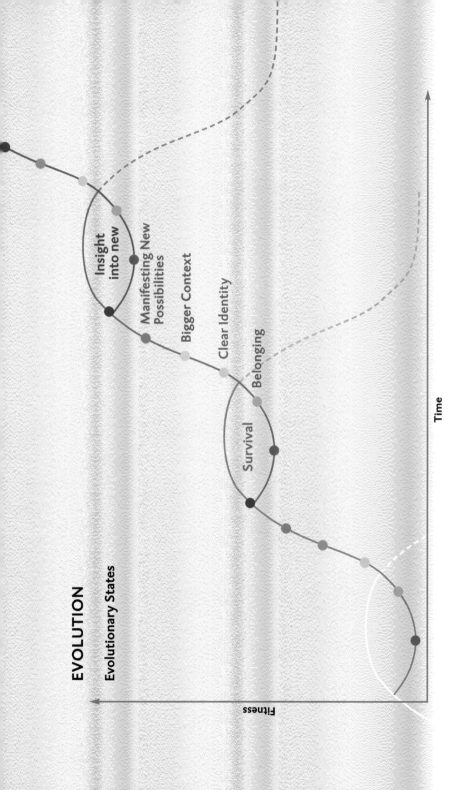

EVOLUTION

Evolutionary States

Insight into new

Manifesting New Possibilities

Bigger Context

Clear Identity

Belonging

Survival

Fitness

Time

into the Gamma trap. Here, stress is at its greatest. We can no longer make sense of our world or our place in it. Depression and anger are common symptoms of the Gamma trap. Our energy is directed against the old system, be it inside ourselves, or in the world around us.

Howard Bloom identifies another useful key element of healthy systems, which he calls "Inner Judges". Our Inner Judges quite literally build us up or wind us down, based on how effective we are being in relation to the whole – how well we fit. If we can't make sense of the whole around us, then our Inner Judges give us a hard time. For cells, this phenomenon is known as programmed cell death: cells are biologically wound down when they are perceived as no longer useful by the system. Since we are made up of cells, it should be no surprise that we get depressed at such times, and sometimes even suicidal.

The arrows arching out from the Gamma trap in Figure 1.9 represent a crazed search for alternatives, as we struggle to find a way out. Howard Bloom calls these "Inter-group Tournaments", as different initiatives try out new ways of doing things, until the collective system settles on one and moves on. It is quite literally a fight for survival. The system may break down at that point. In terms of our individual experience, we may regress to earlier ways of coping, entrenching ourselves in places we have been before. Although this may provide temporary respite, deep down we know that it is not an adequate place to be, and that dissonance will gnaw away at us until we move on again. For an organisation, it often means collapse. For a governance system, it may mean a breakdown into its constituent parts – so a global governance system would regress to inter-nation competition, and a national governance system would break down into its regions or tribes. (This is not the same as subsidiarity,

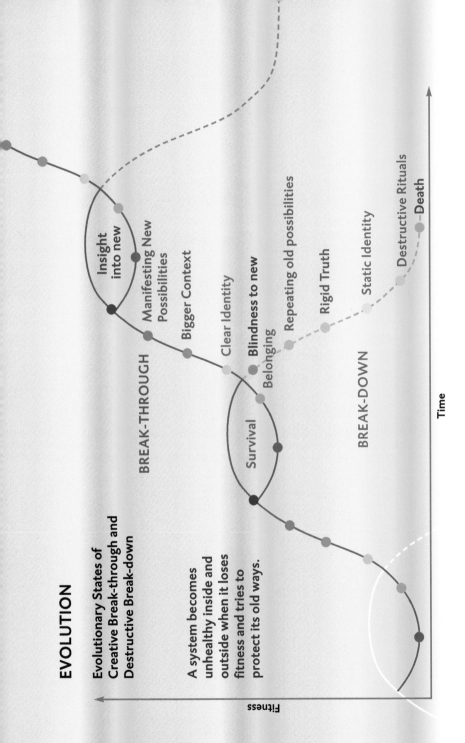

EVOLUTION

Evolutionary States of Creative Break-through and Destructive Break-down

A system becomes unhealthy inside and outside when it loses fitness and tries to protect its old ways.

BREAK-THROUGH

Insight into new

Manifesting New Possibilities

Bigger Context

Clear Identity

Survival

Blindness to new

Belonging

Repeating old possibilities

Rigid Truth

BREAK-DOWN

Static Identity

Destructive Rituals

Death

Fitness

Time

FIGURE 1.8: *Stages of Emergence and Decline*

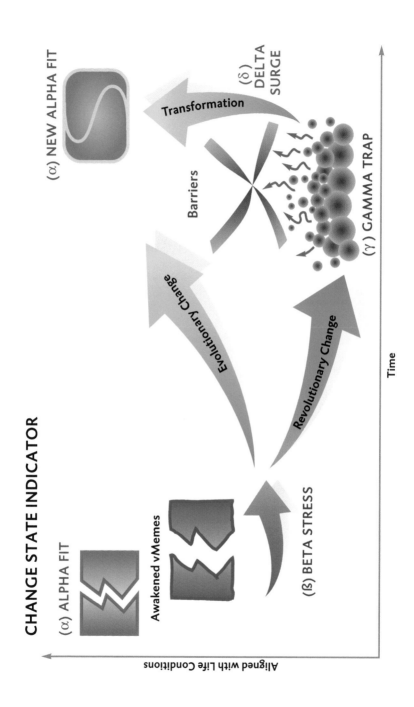

FIGURE 1.9: *Change State Indicator of Clare W. Graves*

where decisions are taken at the most appropriate level, which will often involve some kind of conscious devolution of power. In subsidiarity, the role of the larger governing system is usually somewhat refined, not removed in its entirety).

After much anguish, we may break through the barriers presented by the Gamma trap, releasing into the exuberant energy of the Delta surge. This is an exciting place to be after the depression of the Gamma trap. At last we can see the light! The world makes sense again and we can see how we fit in. From here, we can surge on up to the new Alpha fit. What a relief!

However, the Delta Surge is also a very hazardous stage. The danger lies in the negative energy that we hold towards the old order, our resentment of the barriers we had to fight. We are tempted to turn round to the old order and cut off their heads with a swish of our newly sharpened sword. This is a recipe for trouble later on, which brings us to another key aspect of universal evolutionary tendencies.

Story

It is late autumn 2004. The Netherlands has just undergone the second major shock murder of a public figure in two years. The society was just recovering from the first when the second happened. I am contacted by Dr. Don Beck: "Times like these are when a society is most open to new thinking. Let's do something". We organise a meeting called "The Spiral Dynamics of Fundamentalism". We expect 40 people – more than 200 register. The event is a great success, and at that moment I realise that something is shifting in the collective field of the Netherlands. I decide to form the Dutch node of the Center for Human Emergence (CHE) to act as an attractor for new thinking and practice in the Netherlands. As the old system comes under stress and starts to fall apart, how can we help to put in place the conditions for emergence of the new? I am trembling inside at the thrill of trying to embody everything I have been reading and talking about in recent years, and at the realisation that this is going to be as much an inner journey for me as an outer journey for the organisation and society. And it feels deeply right – almost as if I have no choice in the matter. In Spring 2005, the CHE Netherlands is legally registered.

Inclusion or Repression

As we dissociate from an old way of doing things (be it an internal value system or an external organisation), we need to differentiate the new from the old. We need to put some distance between the new way of doing things and the old way. It is a natural process: the push against the old which gives rise to the new.

It is a very delicate moment. For a healthy transition to occur, we must not only transcend the old, but also include the best of it in the new (see Wilber 2000). Once we have differentiated from the old, we need to re-embrace the healthy parts of the old system and bring them into the new. After all, the old system initially emerged to solve some problems and must have succeeded in doing so well enough for us now to be in a place where we are ready to move on.

Unfortunately, what often happens is that the new system not only differentiates out the old one, but goes a step further and dissociates itself from it. Instead of transcending and including, it transcends and represses. In doing so, it is actually repressing a core part of its compound self, as the old system must be part of the "new" individual or organisation in order for us to have got to where we are. Repression leads to various forms of pathology in the individual or collective – the form will depend on the particular phase that was repressed (see Wilber's Integral Psychology for a thorough analysis of this in the individual, and his Up from Eden for a far-reaching and enlightening look at how this plays out in our collective cultural and civilisational evolution).

The dynamic of transcend-and-include versus transcend-and-repress is a core part of the landscape of evolutionary systems. Evolutionary Leaders do their utmost to foster the conditions for transcendence and inclusion: no easy task, as it requires great depths of compassion (see Chapter 2).

Directionality of Evolution

I referred briefly to this concept in the introduction. The basic idea is that there is directionality to evolution. The difference between direction and directionality is that direction suggests that evolution is trying to reach a place, whereas directionality suggests more the trends that it is following as it unfolds. Those trends are of increasing exterior complexity and increasing interior compassion.

Ever since the big bang, the universe has been arranging itself in ever-higher orders of complexity at the same time as it has been expanding ever faster. The ordering involves parts coming together into greater wholes. So from hydrogen, there eventually emerged human beings, along a path of gradual transcending and including. For example, atoms are transcended and included by molecules, which are in turn transcended and included by cells, which are in turn transcended and included by multi-cellular organisms. It is clear that each new level must be more complex in its nature than the previous ones, as it has transcended and included them. As each new level emerges, it also further refines the relationships between the levels and between the parts at each level, creating a higher order and more efficient role distribution. So in a way, this increasing complexity also creates increasing simplicity.

The fact that each new level transcends and includes the previous ones also means that its embrace is wider – that is to say, it includes more of the universe within its whole (cells contain more than molecules, which contain more than atoms). From an interior perspective, we could call this greater embrace greater compassion. It can be hard to relate compassion to atoms, molecule or cells, so let's look instead at human consciousness.

As our awareness develops from birth, it expands out from being focused purely on our own self, to those immediately surrounding us, to various forms of group we identify with (from football club or music sub-culture, to regions or nations), and then, if the conditions are right, on to an awareness of ourselves as part of the global family of human beings and potentially even all sentient beings, all the way to awareness of ourselves as part of the universe – and outwards, as more continues to unfold. Each emerging stage – from ego-centric to ethno-centric to world-centric to universe-centric – transcends and includes the previous ones, thus widening its awareness and embrace, identifying with ever more of the universe, and therefore able to feel compassion for an expanding circle of life.

It is important to add that although we can notice this directionality, firstly we have no guarantee that any form of life will continue on in this way at any particular point (it can always break down) and, secondly, we have no idea what the surface manifestation will be of these deeper stages. At each moment we are co-creating the future with the rest of the universe. There is no pre-determined path. As we struggle with the challenges that are our particular inheritance, we create the patterns for the solutions of the future. It happens in the present, with every thought and feeling we have and every action that we take. The responsibility we carry is no less than that. The diversity of forms that these different levels can take is as vast as the number of beings who inhabit them. So we find common patterns at the deep level, with a rich diversity of forms on the surface.

An understanding and realisation of directionality is important because it gives us a sense of our context and the path we are walking. It helps us to understand our own journey and the journeys of others. Nobody can be forced to shift levels. Everyone has their own tasks in life. We can simply help to nurture the conditions under which everyone can flourish for the good of the whole, whilst keeping the path open for those who are ready to take the next step.

SUMMARY

We have identified the following universal evolutionary tendencies:

- The dance between yang wholeness-identity and yin partness-belonging.

- The change cycle (the Adizes life-cycle, the S-curve and the change states).

- The dynamic of transcend and include or transcend and repress.

- The five elements of Conformity Enforcement, Diversity Generation, Resource Shifters, Inner Judges and Inter-group Tournaments.

- The directionality of increasing complexity and compassion.

Evolutionary Leadership includes at its core an understanding and feeling for these dynamics. Taken together, they provide a broad picture of the way evolutionary systems work (that includes us and our contexts!). They are the wider canvas onto which we can start to paint the more specific situation that we find ourselves in today, as significant parts of planet Earth.

CHAPTER TWO

Where We're At

Build the Arks (King Kong Song)

My sisters and brothers from other mothers,
We are the ones
Where the oceans meet the shore,
We are the ones
We have been waiting for.

I just read about the coming of the ice age
Earth's rage
The mighty mother, the sage,
 Turning another page
Of evolution
A natural solution
The vibration
Of creation
Melting ice caps into the gulf stream flows
The European heating system blows
Beyond repair
My mother, father, sister, brother live there
Stop, bear witness, take a long good stare
Digest our reality and start to care
The planet is movin' on
We all be livin' in the final swan song
The future's comin' on strong
Like King Kong
We all be the hapless maiden

Looking in his big brown eyes
Beginning to realise
It's all beyond our control
Bigger than we'll ever be
See?
Fuck the swan song,
This is the King Kong song
We ain't got no choice but to go along.

No more prizes for predicting the rain
The pain
New starts
Time to build the arks

What's my contribution
At this crazy time?
Am I gonna whine?
Complain
About the pain?
The fact we all seem to be going insane?
No!
Trust in surprise
Integrity has no compromise
Release all ties
Open the eyes.

Our survival seems hit and miss
Like the world is taking the piss
A final good night kiss
All this material wealth
The illusion of bliss
It's a big mis–stake
Time to rake

The fallen leaves
Autumn choices
Winter bereaves
Not everyone will make it
We can't fake it
There's no hiding
From this colliding
With the end of an era
It's never been clearer
Some will get left behind
Linger in our minds
Their remains to find
In millions of years
As we learn again our evolution
From homo-confusion
To Homo-luminum

No more prizes for predicting the rain
The pain
New starts
Time to build the arks

Gather now at our community centres
With friends and mentors
And Elders
We all be the welders
Of fragmentation
On the edges of the new creation
The builders of the New Space Station
Right here in the arms of the mother
Where the heroes gather undercover
Sensing the future with sonar sound
The builders of boats abound

Readying for the coming storms
Trainers of the warriors who break the norms
Yield to the field
Drop the shield

What are the skills we need to survive?
To be one of the ones alive
Who looks back
Thinking
"holy shit how did we survive that?"
What does it take to make the warrior caste
To see our king kong future comin' on fast
Then look back and know it as the past?

This ain't about seekin' thrills
We need to know the survival skills
Get into training
I'm not exaggerating
I wish I was
This is real,
now
here
It's time to get clear.

There's no more prizes for predicting the rain
The pain
New starts
It's time to build the arks

(BY TIM MERRY)

Having looked at the broad context of how the parts and wholes of the universe fit together and co-evolve, it is time to get closer to home. We are in a critical phase in our evolution as *homo sapiens sapiens* and as the planet Earth.

As Ervin Laszlo (2001) has described it, we have come through a Trigger Phase as technological innovation has enabled us to manipulate the Earth's resources more efficiently for our own ends. This in turn lead to a Transformation Phase in which these innovations irreversibly changed our social and environmental relations, creating greater resource production, faster population growth, greater societal complexity and an increasing impact on our social and natural environment. All of which has lead to the Critical Phase in which our old ways of doing things are proving inadequate to the challenges we are facing, and we are searching for more adequate ways of organising ourselves that will fit better into our larger context. We are reaching the point where we either break through or break down.

So, on the broad canvas of universal evolutionary tendencies, how do we illustrate our current situation? What is the more specific evolutionary context of the Critical Phase we now find ourselves in?

To explore this, I will be using one particular map of the landscape to help us situate where we are. It is a map of our evolutionary context, called Spiral Dynamics Integral. There are many different maps out there, of varying depth and clarity (see the back of Ken Wilber's *Integral Psychology* for a long comparative list of maps of developmental stages in the Self, in our cognition, in our morals and in our socio-cultural contexts). Spiral Dynamics Integral goes a good way up and quite far down, and can be linked in across all four quadrants (Self, Organism, Webs of Culture, Systems and Structures). The colour code gives it an easy language to engage with. This is also the map that I am most familiar with and have explored and tested most thoroughly. As ever, this is an introduction to the essence of this map, and if it intrigues you I would strongly encourage you to look at it in greater depth yourself.

First, it is useful to remind ourselves of our bigger context. This is the evolutionary journey we have been on so far:

Our Evolutionary Story

From www.the great story.com with kind permission

   I Great Radiance – 13.7 billion yrs ago
  II Galactic phase – begins 12 billion yrs ago
 III Hadean early Earth, pre-life – begins 4.6 billion years ago (bya)
 IV Archean first bacteria – begins 3.8 bya
  V Proterozoic amoebas – begins 2 bya
 VI Paleozoic Era of complex life – begins 540 million years ago (mya)
      540-500 mya Cambrian
      500-440 mya Ordovician
      440-410 mya Silurian
      410-360 mya Devonian
      360-290 mya CarbonifeousS
      290-245 mya Permian
VII Mesozoic Era (Age of Dinosaurs) 245 mya
      245-210 mya Triassic
      210-45 mya Jurassic
      145-65 mya Cretacious
VIII Cenzoic Era (Mammals & Birds) 65 mya

Figure 2.1 shows the big picture of the nested hierarchy within which our human civilisation is unfolding. A nested hierarchy (also known as a "holarchy", where the "holons" which make it up are both wholes and parts) is what results when we summarise the universal trends in evolutionary systems that we explored in Chapter 1. Each emerging system is born out of the previous one, and thus transcends and includes it. The reason the model is pyramid-shaped is that the breadth of each stratum represents "span", which simply means how widespread that particular system is. It is obvious that the universe system will always be more widespread than the solar system, which is more widespread than our atmosphere, and so on. So the greater the depth, the less the span. The atmosphere has transcended and included more than the solar system has transcended and included, so it has greater depth. And there will always be more solar system than atmosphere.

Another core trend we identified earlier was the directionality of increasing complexity and embrace. Complexity increases with depth. The make-up of our atmosphere is more complex than the solar system out of which it emerged: it is composed of more elements which it has to hold together in order to perform its task.

These trends also apply to our human systems. Figure 2.2 focuses in on the top two levels represented in Figure 2.1 (anthroposphere and civilisation), and illustrates in more detail the human journey. Remember that the same evolutionary principles apply: we are the unfolding universe.

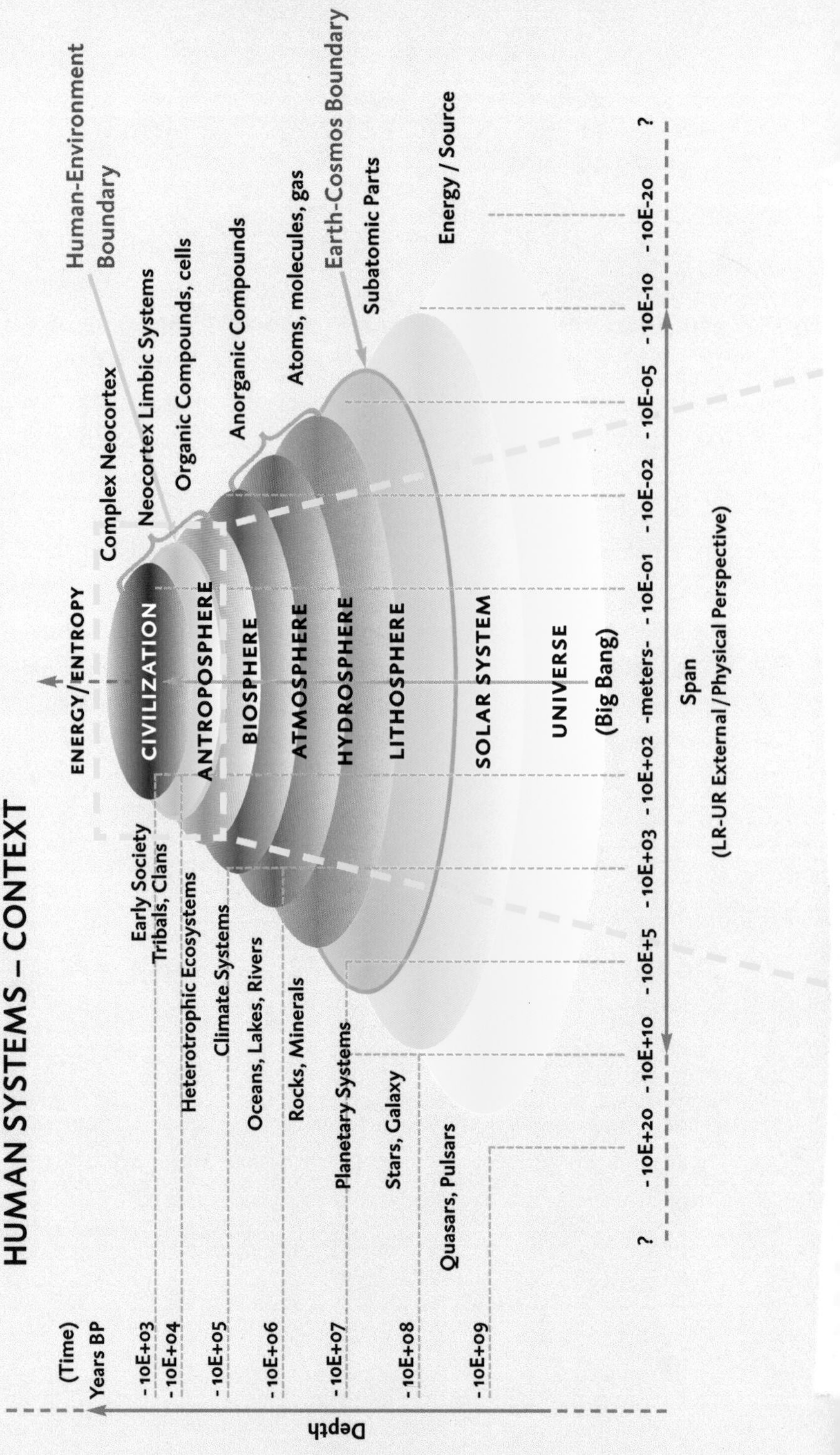

FIGURE 2.1: *Nested Hierarchy of Evolution*

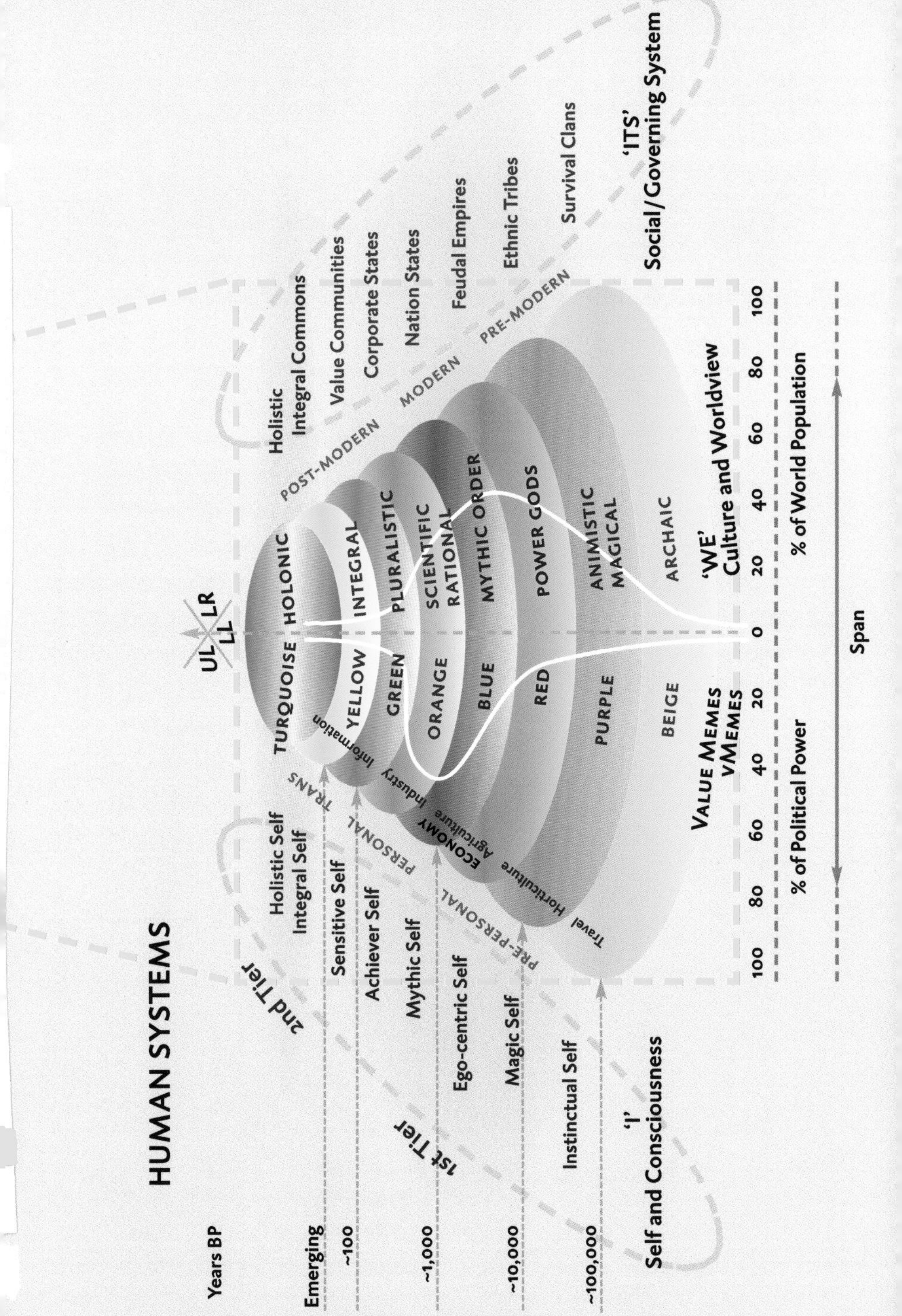

FIGURE 2.2: *Human Evolution*

Up the different sides of the pyramid you can see three of Wilber's four quadrants. On the left is the I-Self, going from pre-personal to personal to trans-personal. In the centre is the We-Cultures and on the right the Its-systems, stretching from pre-modern to modern to post-modern. The It-Organism is round the back – we will look at it more closely in Chapter 4.

Again, the shape of the graphic in Figure 2.2 represents relative span and depth, as in Figure 2.1 showing the physical universe. There will always be more of the lower systems present than the higher systems, as we have to pass through the lower systems to get to the higher ones, and in doing so we transcend and include them. So lower levels of consciousness will still be present in our system as the higher ones unfold. There will always be more of the lower levels in the world than higher levels – even if they are not active or "lit up".

This map can also be summarised as in the table below, with the forms that each level takes in the different quadrants. The table includes Clare Graves' original code that he assigned to each level. The colour codes were added by Don Beck and Christopher Cowan to give us an easier language with which to work. Table 2.1 starts at Beige, the lowest level on the graphic above.

In what follows, I will use the colour code to refer to the developmental waves set out in the table, which co-evolve in all four quadrants. We can see the same deep pattern arise in our individual consciousness, in our physical organism and behaviour, in our collective consciousness and in our collective systems and structures.

This, then, is our collective evolutionary story. Our individual consciousness, collective worldviews and civilisational forms are

LEVEL 1st Tier	GRAVES CODE	I –SELF	WE –CULTURE	ITS –STRUCTURES
Beige	Express self for physiological survival	Instinctual Self	Archaic	Survival Clans
Purple	Sacrifice self to maintain the ways of old	Magic Self	Animistic-magical	Ethnic Tribes
Red	Express self impulsively at any cost without shame or fear	Ego-centric Self	Power Gods	Feudal Empires
Blue	Sacrifice self for reward later	Mythic Self	Mythic Order	Nation States
Orange	Express self for self-gain, but calculatedly	Achiever Self	Scientific Rational	Corporate States
Green	Sacrifice self to get acceptance now	Sensitive Self	Pluralistic	Value Communities
2nd Tier				
Yellow	Express self with concern for, and not at the expense of, others	Integral Self	Integral	Integral Commons
Turquoise	Sacrifice self to existential reality	Holistic Self	Holonic	Holistic

TABLE 2.1: *Spiral Dynamic Stages and Color Code*

co-evolving in interaction with each other. All those which we have already passed through are still present in our system, because we have transcended and included (or repressed) them. Others are still forming.

Each stage or wave is more complex than the previous one, as it includes the past in its present make-up. Each includes more of life in its embrace, moving from ego-centric to ethno-centric to world-centric and beyond. This does not make one stage better than any other. When we are born in the material world, we start at Beige. We do not criticise young children for not yet being at a more complex level – it is part of their natural development. In fact, if we do not nurture the earlier systems carefully, we damage the very path that has got us to where we are, thereby creating a very unhealthy situation in ourselves and others. Criticising or attacking earlier systems would be like cells attacking the molecules which compose them, or the neo-cortex brain deciding to cut out the reptilian brain on which it rests: a suicidal path. Unfortunately, as we will soon see, this is precisely what often happens.

Before summarising the story, here are a few things to keep in mind:

- The four quadrants co-evolve, so that our interior consciousness evolves in interaction with the life conditions around us, triggered by our awareness of a world that is beyond our current capacity for sense-making and which demands new systems of understanding.

- There are normally three systems gathered around the centre of gravity at any one time: an old one which is "exiting", a dominant one, and a new one which is "entering". All the older systems are still there, in the cellar ready to be lit up if the conditions so warrant.

- Each emergent system transcends and includes the previous ones: it emerges out of them.

- The general directionality is towards increasing exterior complexity and interior compassion.

- No one system is better than another

- Stress happens when there is a lack of fit across quadrants.

- Evolutionary Leadership is about facilitating the conditions for people to live healthily wherever they are in their development, and to nurture e*mergence when the time is ripe.*

We pick up the story at Beige. The Instinctual Self emerges in a world where survival is the driving force. All our energy goes into staying alive. Heads down with our work cut out. Once this basic need has been met, we raise our heads and become aware of others around us and of the natural environment that we are part of (Purple). Driven by the need for safety, we bond together in tribes to enhance our survival. Sensing greater forces at play around us, we develop rituals to appease them. In this pre-personal phase, we still feel one with our environment – we are still in unconscious union. On the cusp of the moment where the mind emerges out of the body, we give mental meaning to events still in the nature-body realm. With the new basic structure of mind just emerging, it is a time of mysticism and new sensations.

Now that the need for safety has been met, a major transition occurs. Wham bam: here comes our ego and sense of self (Red). Emerging out of the pre-personal union with our environment, the egocentric self bursts on to the scene, conscious for the first time of its existence as a unique entity. With the world looking like a threatening jungle, we become the Power Gods who will tame it. Where previously there were nature gods, I am now the God, with my lieutenants in tow, and others following along submissively. It is a phase with great energy, the power to break old patterns and shatter boundaries – truly transformative power. In its healthiest form, Red successfully transcends and includes Purple, keeping a sense of connection to the natural world from which it emerged. If it goes beyond differentiation and dissociates, it cuts itself off from its original context. In separation, the mind represses the body that holds it.

This mind/body split is a major source of our current problems, particularly in the Western context. It has allowed us to rape the natural world from which we emerged, to mine the very foundations of our existence. In doing so, we are deeply wounding ourselves. It is no surprise that there is so much trauma in the world, with this dynamic at play. Deep healing is needed in ourselves and in our interaction with the world. As we become aware of the pain this split has caused us, it is also important not to swing the other way and repress the Red system in ourselves. In its healthy form it plays an essential part in our evolution.

---

* The terms "express-self" and "sacrifice-self" originate from the initial work of Professor Clare Graves, who discovered and articulated the systems which currently make up the stages of the Spiral.

At this point, it is useful to highlight a core dynamic at work. It is one we have met before: the dance between yin and yang. As you can see in the graphics, the colours of the Spiral Dynamics systems alternate between warm and cool colours. The warm colours represent "express-self" systems, and the cool colours represent "sacrifice-self" systems*. Express-self systems are characterised by the drive to go out and fit the world to ourselves (yang). Sacrifice-self systems are characterised by a drive to fit ourselves into the world (yin). The dance manifests as an upward spiral between these two poles.

As we get enough of one side, we feel the pull back to the other side. But we don't go back to the system we came from, because our consciousness has been upgraded by the new complexity of the previous system. Once Red has emerged, for example, we know that Purple is inadequate, so we need to seek for another form of sacrifice-self which transcends *and includes* both Red and Purple. That is Blue. The difference between Purple (sacrifice-self) and Blue (also sacrifice-self) is Red.

Red has introduced hierarchy into the system (ideally with itself at the top). Blue is a sacrifice-self response to that. The drive for the sacrifice-self system is to adapt oneself to the world. If we are to fit ourselves into a hierarchical world, then there must be some greater force out there which rules over us, allowing us to lord it over others. This is precisely what Blue creates: mythic Order, with a belief in One Greater Truth. The only problem is that there can be only *one* truth, and given that this system emerges in many different cultural contexts, a wide diversity of One Truth belief systems manifest, all competing and clashing with each other (one need look no further than the dynamics in the Middle East today).

Blue has introduced a sense of guilt, being rewarded later for good behaviour now. This colours the express-self energy of Red to create Orange: "express-self for self gain, calculatedly". The yang energy returns again, but this time with a more subtle strategy than Red. The Achiever Self rebels against the One-Truth doctrines of Blue, and senses a world out there full of opportunity. No one tells *me* what to believe, I will head out into the wide world and work it out for myself. The scientific-rational collective mindset heads out to explore and discover the world and all its potential. And I will be the best at whatever I choose to do.

The emergence of this system coincided in the West with the industrial revolution and free market capitalism. They are of course perfect vehicles for Achiever-Self energy. However, it is important to remember that they are only surface manifestations of the deeper Orange code. Orange does not equal industrialisation. Orange equals "express-self for self gain, calculatedly". So people in cultures where Orange is yet to emerge will not necessarily have to adopt the same surface models as we did in the West. In fact, a core part of evolutionary leadership at the global level will be to find and facilitate the emergence of more healthy expressions of Orange for the good of the whole. A system always has a healthy intention, namely to solve an emergent set of new challenges. Unhealthy expressions develop only when a system tries to impose its value system onto other systems, or when its activities damage the greater whole (the global commons, such as water, air, soil and so on).

Orange has indeed run its course in the industrialised countries. It has gone beyond its healthy limit and is currently polluting the collective space. Creating the conditions for the emergence of Yellow via Green, whilst doing what we can to protect the collective space from Orange's adolescent expansionism, is a major task for evolutionary leaders today.

Orange introduces diversity into the system, in the form of multiple opportunities and choices. It liberates the individual from collective tyranny. Green takes that wonderful diversity and adds a sacrifice-self energy – "Sacrifice self to fit in now". Green reacts against Orange's race to the top, and in looking for a way to fit back into the world, it settles on principles of egalitarianism and tolerance of the other. Green takes the diversity that Orange has introduced and applies it with the perspective that everyone has their own truth, no one can tell anyone else what to do, and we must respect each other and our differences. If all truth is relative, then who am I to stand up and proclaim that I have a truth? Sacrifice-self to fit in. This creates a great energy for liberating others from oppression – people as well as other beings in the natural world.

Green then in turn reaches its own limits, and this is a key transition point. For this moment is not only a shift from one system to the next, but a shift to a whole new level, or "tier". Graves (2002) reckoned from his research that these systems were gathered in tiers of six, and expected there to be three tiers in total. So the shift from Green to Yellow is also a shift from first to second tier. This is what Graves called "a momentous leap for mankind". His justification for this was the extraordinary jump he found in the data at this point. Yellow and Turquoise showed levels of complexity that were a quantum leap above Green and the other first-tier systems.

The major shift is that first tier systems find it hard to relate to worldviews other than their own (even Green, which preaches tolerance, will only really tolerate those who also believe in tolerance). First-tier systems attack each other either as old-fash-

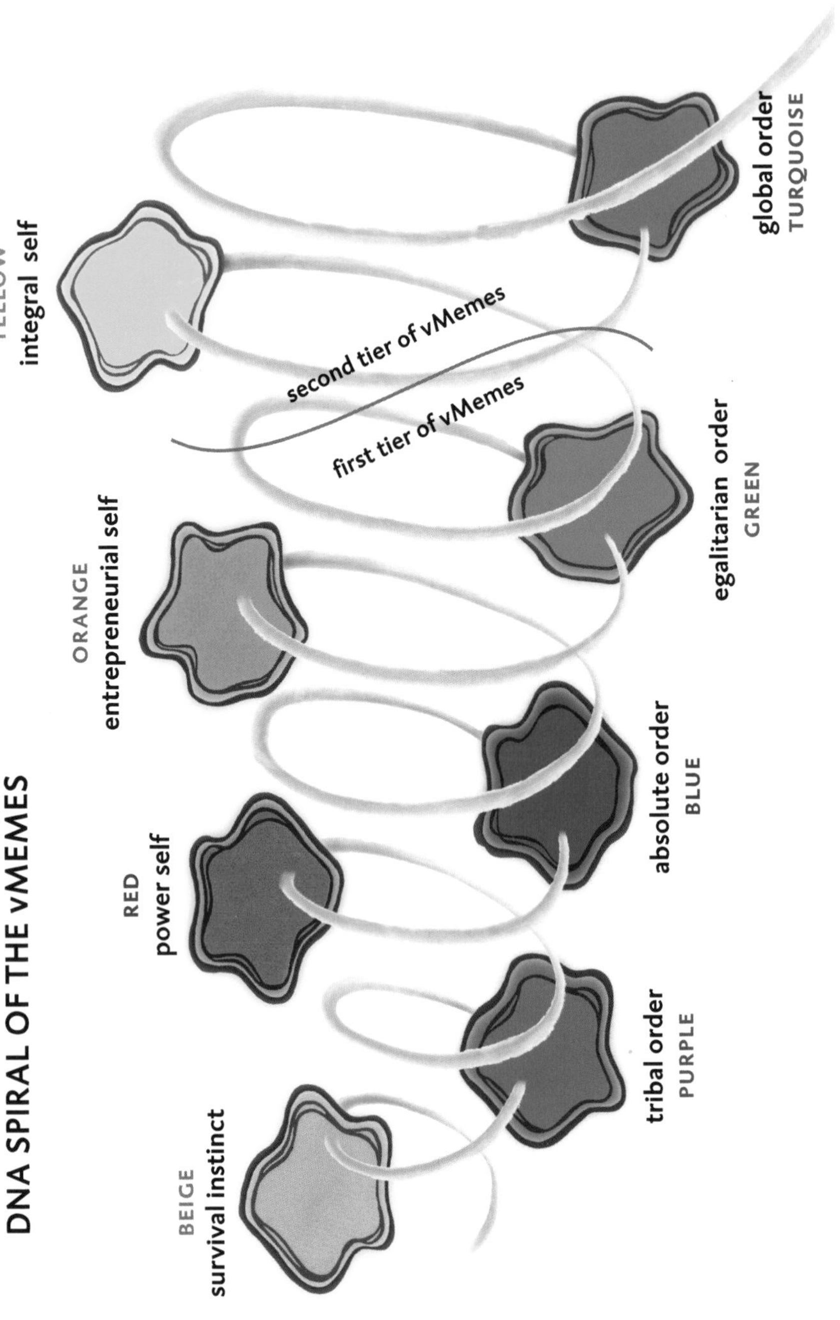

DNA SPIRAL OF THE vMEMES

YELLOW integral self

TURQUOISE global order

ORANGE entrepreneurial self

second tier of vMemes

first tier of vMemes

GREEN egalitarian order

RED power self

BLUE absolute order

BEIGE survival instinct

PURPLE tribal order

FIGURE 2.3: *DNA Spiral of the vMemes*

ioned and behind the times, or as idealistic and a threat to traditional ways. Second-tier systems begin to see how the whole links up together in a developmental context, understanding that each level has an essential role to play. Given the understanding of developmental depth, second-tier systems are able to engage with the world as it really is, with all its deep diversity, rather than as we would ideally like it to be.

As an example, Green may expect and demand of people centred in Red that they sit in circle, share their feelings and show respect for everyone present. However, given that this context does not meet the evolutionary need of those in Red, stress and disorder are likely to result, not because of the nature of the Red system itself, but because of the lack of fit between the people and the context. Red needs a healthy hierarchy with clear rules and order within which to express itself. Blue, not Green, is the next system for Red.

So the second-tier imperative becomes to meet people where they are, to help create the conditions where everyone can be most fully themselves in a way that benefits the whole, and to gently facilitate emergence when people are ready to move on.

The six second-tier systems seem to have parallels with the first-tier systems. Beige, the first system in the first tier, is occupied with survival of the individual. Yellow, the first system in the second tier, is also triggered by survival concerns, but this time for the survival and wellbeing of the whole of humanity and the planet. Like Beige, Yellow tends to keep its head down and get on with doing what needs to be done, but in a way that understands and respects where people are at, and the bigger context within which their work is happening.

Yellow has introduced the idea of unity and interrelationship. Turquoise takes this into the sacrifice-self realm, with "sacrifice-self to existential realities" (the code Graves originally assigned to this system). What does this actually mean? It means "accept what is". This is of course at the heart of many spiritual teachings. In the same way that Purple was mystical, Turquoise is also mystical, but at a new level. Purple was mystical due to the emerging mind in the world of the body and matter. Turquoise is mystical due to emerging soul in the world of mind. It senses deep interconnectedness – the fullness and emptiness that seem to underlie everything when we really feel that we are part of a whole in which everything is connected. Energy flows between everything and binds it together. It is the ground for a new sense of being.

Turquoise is the most complex pattern that Graves could identify during his research in the 1970s. Since then, I am aware of at least two more systems that have come onto our collective radar screens: Coral and Teal. The reason why these seem to have emerged so quickly is that *the rate of change in the world is increasing exponentially.* That is quite a concept to take on board. Ray Kurzweil points out that it means that the whole of the 20th century was like twenty years of change at today's rate, and that in the next twenty years we will make five times the progress that we saw in the 20th century. With an exponentially increasing rate of change, it should be no surprise that we are witnessing the emergence of Coral and Teal already.

Coral is the second-tier equivalent of first-tier Red. Red's code is "express-self without fear or shame" for the sake of the ego-centric self. One could use the same code for Coral: express-self without fear or shame, but for the good of the whole. Coral, like Red, is an extremely powerful and transformative system. It is the birth of the self beyond ego. As three systems are normally at play within us at time (the exiting, the dominant and the entering), when Coral emerges it is the first time that we are fully free from the energy of the first tier: Green fades out, with Yellow, Turquoise and Coral now active.

Teal, like Blue, is about order, but instead of ethno-centric order and truth, it is about universal order and truth. It finds ways to understand the universe that take into account all that we know so far, without exclusion. Because to exclude something would be to deny part of our greater selves. Teal dedicates itself to service of that greater whole.

Story

Meanwhile, back at the CHE... Following on from the Spiral Dynamics of Fundamentalism event, we organise another event to launch the CHE in the early summer of 2005. A core part of what we have to offer initially is an integral overview of the dynamics around Dutch society and fundamentalism. The value systems that motivated the murders were primarily Red warrior energy, with a thin skin of Blue traditional. The political and media classes in the Netherlands tend to have a lot of Green post-modern. The clash of Red and Green is the primary value-memetic story around these murders and how society was grappling with the implications.

Green finds it very hard to judge anything as right or wrong, as it likes to include everything and find a contextual reason for it (eg "the murderers were repressed by society, so we had it coming"). Yet this was clearly an inadequate response, and had already been exposed in politically-correct attempts to justify the attacks on the twin towers on 11 September 2001. The Green system was being confronted with issues of developmental depth, something it finds very hard to see and value.

Questions such as "tolerance is all very well, but should we tolerate intolerance?" shake the very foundations of that value system.

During the period that followed in the Netherlands, we saw the Green value system put under great stress, which led to some of parts of the system regressing to an earlier Blue traditionalist standpoint ("we have Dutch values and norms and everyone should adopt them") whilst other parts set out on a quest for a way to integrate the justifiable criticism of the Green system without jettisoning the valuable contribution of the post-modern mind and culture – creating early signs of an emerging integral Yellow. It was in this context that we positioned the CHE to exert an upward pull towards second tier thinking and action.

Evolutionary Leadership comes from second-tier perspectives. What we need in the world right now are leaders who can see the complexity and the deep patterns, who are no longer attached to their own ego-driven needs for fame or success, but whose life and work is totally in service of the evolving whole. Evolutionary leaders are the people who will be able to heal the wounds that have been and continue to be created by warring systems insisting that their worldview is the only right one. By understanding the dynamics related to these deep systemic codes, we can heal from the bottom up, rather than trying to patch over the surface wounds. By helping to create the conditions that fit people's needs at whatever stage they find themselves, we can significantly lessen stress and conflict, allowing people to follow the path they are on. At the same time, we hold the bigger picture of our planet's collective needs, making sure that meeting the present needs of people and cultures not only doesn't *damage* our global collective space, but actually *enhances* it.

As evolutionary leaders, we look to facilitate healthy expressions of the different systems, as opposed to unhealthy expressions, which would be defined as any expression which limits the expression and development of another system. In other words, a healthy expression facilitates the dynamics of the spiral, while an unhealthy one obstructs it. It is important to remember that the systems themselves are neither healthy nor unhealthy – they just are. It is their surface expressions in behaviour which can be categorised as more or less healthy.

If we succeed in transcending and including the first-tier systems at the global level, then both the identity of those first-tier systems and the quality of the global community will be enhanced. In this work, there can be no compromise. No one should have to compromise their deeper needs for the good of the whole, otherwise we are not properly transcending and including. This should give us the ability to "light up" the appropriate system in a healthy way at the appropriate time – what we might call "full spectrum capacity"*.

If we are to be able to do this in our work in the world, we must have come to terms with and integrated all the first-tier systems in ourselves. Only if we have a healthy relationship to the Spiral within us can we work in a healthy way with the Spiral in the world. So it is important to notice which of the first-tier systems we may feel some resistance to or rejection of, and to work on integrating them in ourselves.

There is another reason why the emergence of Coral is so important. Real passion and clarity seems to be present primarily in

---

* See the work of Richard Barrett (1998) for a map that is similar to Spiral Dynamics. He coined the term "full spectrum" to mean having all the systems available.

the two central systems of each tier – Red and Blue in the first tier and Coral and Teal in the second tier. The first two systems (e.g. Beige/Purple and Yellow/Turquoise) are still emerging into the tier, and the two later systems (e.g. Orange/Green) are relativising and on their way out. In the world today, people seem again to be yearning for a sense of purpose and greater truth. For the moment, the only people who are really offering that are the radical, often extremist, movements centred in ethno-centric Red and Blue. These systems are by their nature exclusivist and inimical to all those who do not subscribe to their truth (e.g. fundamentalist religious movements, be they Christian, Islamic or Jewish). These movements are attracting people because they offer such clear meaning and passion, in a world which has otherwise lost its moral compass in so many ways.

It is only when Coral emerges that passion and purpose can once more blaze onto the scene. Coral has a mission and will stand in the fire to make it happen. Coral dares once more to take a stand on what is right and wrong, because it feels compelled by the universe surging through its veins. Clarity is once more at a premium – clarity that helps us to see how things hang together, that holds up a mirror to our own ego games, and calls us into our higher selves. No compromise. Evolve or die, as Barbara Marx Hubbard says.

At the same time, beneath this passion and clarity of purpose is a lightness and an understanding informed by the Turquoise realisation that fundamentally all is very well. We will explore this more in Chapter 3.

This shift from first to second tier will be the focus of the next four chapters. In each of the quadrants, what does it mean to change from a first-tier perspective to a second-tier perspective?

The Spiral Dynamics Integral model gives us a map of our evolutionary landscape, helping us to situate ourselves and others in the deeper emergent patterns of our own journeys. It helps us to visualise a new perspective. It provides a tool for understanding the context within which we are called to work. It also implies a huge dose of humility, accompanied by the excitement of once more having a way to make sense of our world.

As Don Beck is fond of saying: "No more prizes for predicting the rain. Only prizes for building the arks". Let's get on with it.

SUMMARY

We are part of an evolutionary dance which involves:

- Change being the only constant.

- A journey that is about 13.7 billion years old as far as we currently know.

- Continually emerging patterns in the ways we think, feel, act, commune and organise.

- New ways that transcend and include the old ways.

- A quantum breakthrough at a certain point (second tier) which allows us to see the whole more clearly and therefore act more consciously.

CHAPTER THREE

Being an Evolutionary Leader

Dalai Lama

I wanna be calmer
Than the Dalai Lama

Like Walden for Henry Thoreau
Livin' at the speed trees grow
Is easier for me
Than
All this information
Diversity
Range of Change
Crazy Complexity
I wanna be free
Live Simply

Follow my heart
Seas Part
If I dare
To be the tortoise and not the hare
Clear the mind
Find
Space
Outside the rat race
See the bigger picture
Outside the rate race
Drink Life's elixir

Follow my heart
Seas Part
If I dare
To be the tortoise and not the hare

Follow my heart
Seas Part
If I dare
To be the tortoise and not the hare

Burnouts and broken minds
Speeding tickets, Life's fines
For being Sebastian Coe
When I should be going slow
Like Billy Whizz and Mr. T
I have lived with my finger on the trigger
I have learnt
From being burnt
Reflection is too important
To leave to chance
Take a stance

Follow my heart
Seas Part
If I dare
To be the tortoise and not the hare
I demand my time
To unwind
Contemplate
See life in a state
Of Clarity
Time out is not Charity
I gotta stop and think

Or life'll be gone in a blink
I'm dead long enough
I'm strong enough
Calling my bluff

I was the hare getting irate
I'm late for a very important date
No passion
Just crashin'
Through life in a haste
What a waste

Follow my heart
Seas Part
If I dare
To be the tortoise and not the hare

For my own sake
Apply the brake
Become awake
From inner peace I can break
The apathy
That had been placed on me
Take responsibility
Fuck career
Become clear
Find a community
True to me
Take off the mute
On the voice of life
Step onto the edge of the knife
Listen for a slice of how life might be
Listen for reality

Follow my heart
Seas Part
If I dare
To be the tortoise and not the hare

I'm not being cute
There's no parachute
We already jumped
Out the plane.
Do we dare to become
Sane
Again?
This ain't about brain
This is about livin'
the future now
Yes is the answer to how

Follow my heart
Seas Part
If I dare
To be the tortoise and not the hare

I will meet you in the field
Beyond right and wrong
That's where I belong
That's where I been all along

(BY TIM MERRY)

In this chapter, we explore what it might feel like to be an evolutionary leader – to lead oneself from a second-tier perspective. This is the Upper Left quadrant of I-Self. As such it is about our interior felt experience. I can do nothing other, therefore, than share with you my own experience of exploring this edge. Along the way, I have come across other people's descriptions which have helped me and which I will also share. Although different people experience this transition in different ways, there do seem to be some common themes. I trust that as I touch on these, you will be able to feel some resonance.

It is important to remember at this point that although what follows is my personal take on this space, it is also our collective story. Given that we are the evolving universe here and now, it is the most impersonal of affairs. What unfolds in any of us as we explore our inner space is the universe unfolding *through* us and *as* us. As such, we cannot claim the credit for the experience, nor can we put ourselves on a pedestal proclaiming that we have discovered the truth all by ourselves. This does not mean that we should not stand up and stand out as the beautiful beings that we are. It is really about how we relate to our experience.

As we explored earlier, the step we have to take is essentially about relationship and connection. It is about transcending our ego's sense of separate self (I use "ego" here and elsewhere to mean our sense of separate self). The development of our sense of unique selfhood has been a key step on our evolutionary path. Now it is time to move on.

In my experience there are two main steps to take, and it seems that one has to come before the other. The first is developing our sense of interconnectedness with everything else. The second is re-engaging with our evolving world whilst resting in the awareness of our deep interconnectedness.

I picture it like a flower. A flower develops roots into the ground before poking its head through into the world. Without its roots it would get blown away and would not survive long, however beautiful it may be. Once it has developed its first roots and started to emerge into the world, its two parts, above the soil and below the soil, reinforce each other. Without the roots, the stem, leaves and petals would have neither food to grow nor stability to stand. Without the leaves to capture the sunlight, the flower would lack the energy to survive. As the flower grows, its roots deepen and its body grows, co-evolving and reinforcing each other.

Likewise, we need to have developed some sense of our deeper ground before we can engage with the world as this new being. Once this is established, our sense of deep connection and our being in the world mutually reinforce each other – the depth of our connectedness and our freedom of being increase together in the spiral dance. Once more we meet the yin and the yang: the yin of connection and the yang of freedom. The step beyond this is when the two exist together in a seamless whole of nondual being.

The Ground of Being

So let us start with the ground. As the Purple system was the ground for us as first-tier beings, Turquoise is the ground for us second-tier beings. Remember Graves' original code: "sacrifice-self to the existential realities". Accept what is. This is the essence of our ground of being.

A number of short statements have helped me to notice the difference between a state where I am not feeling this connection and a state where I am. I came across a flyer from the Impersonal Enlightenment Fellowship which had blazoned across its front cover the two words "stop struggling". They have stayed with me for a long time. For how can we be accepting of what is if we are still struggling? The second statement was from *The Way of the Peaceful Warrior* by Dan Millman (2000): "Stress happens when the mind resists what is". I know I am disconnected from the ground when I catch myself struggling or creating stress.

Everything is the way it is right now and there is nothing we can do to change that. It is what has co-evolved, emerged out of our 13.7 billion-year history. To resist it in any way is to refuse to accept what we are. It also means that we are refusing to see and accept a part of ourselves – for as the co-evolving interconnected whole, we carry it all in us. I am you. I am that. We are one.

A good place to develop this deep sense of connection for me has been in meditation. In stilling myself, in quieting my mind, in connecting to my breath, I feel the stress and struggle fall away. Coming into the present, the connection is simply there. Fundamentally nothing is wrong. All is very well.

What a release. What a relief. All the worries about the way things are in the world, about whether or not I did the right thing earlier in the day, are released. It does not mean I stop caring. It means I stop being obsessed with the past or worried about the future, and am able to see things with far greater clarity as they are now in the present. In fact, the caring and compassion is radically increased. For in feeling the connectedness with everything that is, I not only feel the joy of life, but also all the suffering too. Everyone else's suffering becomes my suffering. I can no longer ignore it, because feeling myself as the world means that the pain of the world is in me too. The tears flow freely as we acknowledge the pain in ourselves. The heart breaks and opens. It is part of our individual and collective healing. Stuart Davis sings "As the tears are tasted, the poison is refined" (*Mercy*).

Connecting to and acknowledging this pain continues to be an important part of my journey. Creating the spaces for others to feel that connection is an important part of evolutionary leadership. Much of it is inspired by the wonderful work of Joanna Macy*, who developed what she calls "despair and empowerment" activities to help people deal with the world they experienced as they engaged in work to remove the threat of nuclear weapons. It continues to be used to great effect to help us come to terms with both the human suffering we are aware of in the world today and the massive environmental destruction and species extinction we are a part of.

Connecting to this deep despair helps to release our immense capacity for compassion, followed by passionate action – hence despair *and* empowerment. There may seem to be a paradox here. How can "accepting what is" live alongside mourning for the way things are? In fact, they go hand in hand. For what is includes pain. The pain and suffering are there, in the world and in us as the world. If we disconnect from it, we are ignoring a core part of what is, and drastically limiting our capacity for compassion. This compassion is not the same as struggling against the way things are. It is opening up to what *is* and allowing ourselves to truly *be* with it. If we start wishing that things

---

* See *People Referenced* for more on Joanna Macy.

were different without accepting the way things are, then we start to lose touch with the ground, to lose our rootedness, and risk being blown away on the winds of idealism.

Our connection to the ground feels and acknowledges the pain whilst at the same time accepting that fundamentally nothing is wrong. This combination allows us to stay connected to who we are and to our greatest compassion, whilst not allowing the compassion that we feel to disempower us from action, knock us off our centre or cloud our clarity. We are able to witness the pain and clearly see the bigger context.

Joanna Macy tells the story of her meeting with Chujow Rinpoche and how he told her of the Shambhala Warriors who emerge when the Earth is in desperate need. They have two main weapons: compassion and insight into the interdependence of all things.

> *"You need both,"* he said. *"Compassion, because it provides the fuel that is the motive power. That is what moves you to engage, to take part in the healing of the world. That openness to the pain of our world is essential. Not to be afraid of it. But by itself it is not enough. By itself it can just burn you up, burn you out. You need the other, you need that insight into the interdependence of all beings and all things. With that you know that the battles we face are not battles between good and evil, but that the line between good and evil runs through the landscape of every human heart. Insight by itself is a cool knowledge; it must be married with the heat of compassion."*
> (MACY & BROWN, 1999)

Sensing the ground of being out of which we all emerge feeds our compassion and insight. It enables us to act from a place of loving stillness and clarity.

Sensing this ground brings with it another seeming paradox. As we feel ourselves to be part of everything else which is, has been and will be, there comes on the one hand a feeling of great fullness and on the other an awareness of great emptiness. There is nothing and there is everything. Sensing the ground transcends this polarity. They are both true. I make sense of it in this way: the everything is all that exists in the whole universe, and the emptiness is that out of which it all emerged 13.7 billion years ago.

It feels like coming home. It feels like I can rest in this great hammock of the universe before it was born. It feels like I belong. It feels like I am loved unconditionally. It feels like coming back to life. I feel.

Story

I am sitting with one of my favourite change agents, from a Dutch government ministry. She is leading a cultural change programme and is deeply committed to an integral vision for the organisation. She looks strained. I have seen her look this way before. I ask her to tell me what's up. The story unfolds, with the tears. The lack of movement she perceives in the organisation is frustrating her again, and making her question whether she is the best person to do this work. My heart opens and the inner smile appears on my face. I tell her my truth – that I see great changes in the organisation and that I don't know of anyone else that could do this in her place. I ask her what she is struggling against. She doesn't fully believe either in herself or in the capacity of others around her. From my deepest sense of the Ground of Being, I invite her to accept that everything is fine just as it is, that everyone, including her, are doing their best, and that that is good enough. She takes a deep sigh, old knowing, and I feel her energy settle back down as her soul resonates with an ancient truth that she has the consciousness to be able to recognise. We help her align her energy with a belief that she has a leadership role to play in this change process, and her system responds well. Things start to align themselves around her in the days that follow.

The Emerging Self

Out of this ground emerges a new being. A being that exists as something far bigger. A being that feels free and whole, unfettered by regrets of the past or fears of the future. A being that is fully alive and engaged in the world as it is. A being of lightness and playfulness, of centeredness and groundedness, of commitment and responsibility. A being who chooses at every moment to do what the universe calls them to do, in full realisation of what is, here and now. What needs to be done next is done with grace and efficiency. A Being, rather than a Doing.

A set of teachings and a discipline that help me to develop this being in myself come from Andrew Cohen and his work on Evolutionary Enlightenment. He has two teaching models (Figure 3.1 and Figure 3.2) that serve to contrast the space where we are still governed by our separate sense of self, which he calls Hell, from the space where we are free from our self-centred ego and connected in deep relationship to all around us, which he calls Heaven.

From the models you can see that the ground of being is permanently present. It is our ever-present awareness. Out of that ground emerges our being. The images remind me of a womb, within which the being develops.

Central to my development have been and continue to be the five tenets, which build onto each other just above the human figure in figure 3.2. The idea is that if we can live by these tenets, the evolutionary impulse naturally emerges. The tenets continue to be of great help to me in my own personal work, and have made a major contribution to my feelings of wholeness and freedom.

1 The first tenet is **Clarity of Intention**. This is about wanting to be free and whole more than anything else. If this is not my primary intention, I have found it all too easy to slip back into self-centredness, using some other need as an excuse. In those situations, I am prioritising something else above my desire to be free and whole. Everything else I do must be set in the context of truly wanting to be free and whole. When working with an affirmation, I have changed it from "I want to be free and whole", because that postpones it to the future – I want it, but I don't have to be it now. What works more effectively for me as an affirmation is "I am free and whole".

2 Next comes the **Law of Volitionality**. This law states that at every moment we have a free choice. We can choose to act from our highest self, or we can choose to be dominated by our ego. This is a big one, as it implies that there can be no excuses. When we truly accept that at every moment we have the choice, then we can't slip into a victim mentality blaming the circumstances or the fact that we may not be feeling at our best that day. We either choose to be free and whole, or not. And if we want it more than anything else, then why would we choose to be anything else? Taking responsibility for that free choice is a key shift.

3 Third up is **Face Everything and Avoid Nothing.** Whenever I introduce this to people, it inevitably triggers a deep breath. It hits home hard. We cannot be free and hide from things at the same time. With the realisation that we are all deeply interconnected as one whole, we know that if we are avoiding something "out there" then we are really avoiding part of our self. It implies great openness and trust, and deep roots into the ground of being. When I manage this, it brings great release and indeed a huge sense of freedom. The world opens up before us, as we open up to the world. Letting life in, we are let into life.

4 Fourth is the **Law of Impersonality.** I have touched on this before. It is another huge one – they are all huge! This law states that all of our experience is impersonal. It is not we as unique and separate individuals who are creating our experiences, but it is the universe unfolding through us and as us. This is a major nail in the ego's coffin. It can no longer claim to be superior to others for having achieved a higher state of personal development. It might not be something that we go around telling others, but we do often tell it to ourselves – which of course determines how we relate to those around us. From a place of detached superiority or engaged compassion? As an affirmation or reminder of this, I use something like "We are the universe unfolding through us". It triggers great humility and centeredness.

5 Finally, **For the Good of the Whole.** This is the end of the road for the ego's separate sense of self. If we have managed to get through the last four with any sense of this work being about personal development for ourselves (which would mean we hadn't fully got the depth of the first four tenets anyway), this finishes it. Due to our deep interconnectedness,

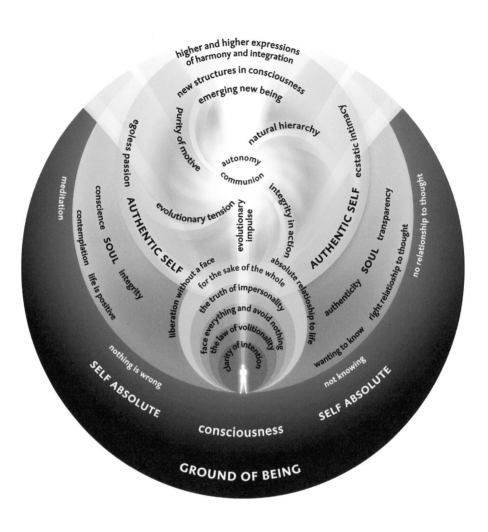

higher and higher expressions
of harmony and integration

new structures in consciousness

emerging new being

purity of motive

natural hierarchy

egoless passion

AUTHENTIC SELF

ecstatic intimacy

autonomy

communion

integrity in action

meditation

conscience

evolutionary tension

evolutionary impulse

absolute relationship to life

transparency

no relationship to thought

contemplation

SOUL

integrity

AUTHENTIC SELF

SOUL

authenticity

right relationship to thought

life is positive

liberation without a face

for the sake of the whole

the truth of impersonality

wanting to know

face everything and avoid nothing

the law of volitionality

clarity of intention

not knowing

nothing is wrong

SELF ABSOLUTE

SELF ABSOLUTE

consciousness

GROUND OF BEING

FIGURE 3.1: *Andrew Cohen and Self – 1*

66

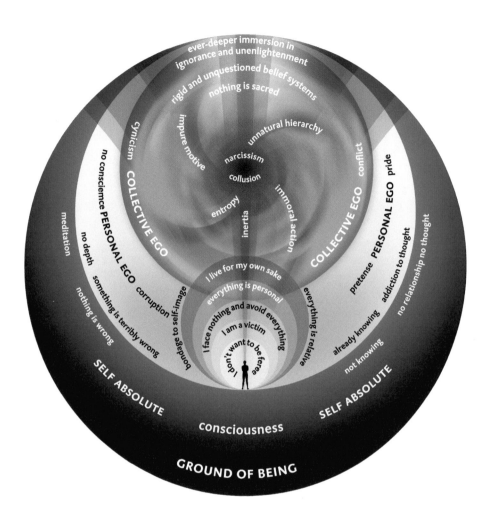

FIGURE 3.2: *Andrew Cohen and Self − 2*

everything we do at every moment has an impact on the greater whole, and therefore on everyone and everything else (*there's* responsibility!). This means that the space I take to work on myself and develop these capacities is not for my sake, as a separate individual perched on my meditation cushion. It is for the good of the whole. For as we develop our own practice in this way, we make it easier for others to be that way too. We are clarifying the patterns of a new way of being, digging the grooves, clearing the path.

The science of this is emerging in the work around the Zero Point Field and Morphogenetic Fields – which show how an energy field which links everything up is both our collective memory bank of the past and our emerging future. Everything we do has an impact on this field, and everything we manifest comes out of it. It is simply a more subtle form of energy, that becomes denser and grosser in the visible world. For more on this, see the work of Lynne McTaggart and Rupert Sheldrake. The point of this final tenet is that all that we do has an impact on the whole, so we should be guided to act for the good of the whole and not be sabotaged by the ego's story about personal development for its own sake.

In my experience, these five tenets help us to become second-tier evolutionary leaders. The Heaven graphic (Figure 3.2) illustrates how the "evolutionary impulse" emerges out of the five tenets, leading to a dance of four core elements swirling around a centre of communion and autonomy (our old friends yin and yang). This centre is the space in which both our autonomy as free individuals and our communion with the planetary and universal whole are radically enhanced, mutually reinforcing each other.

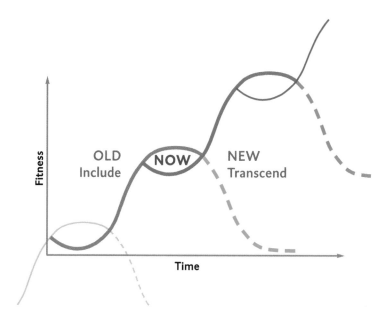

FIGURE 3.3: *Evolutionary Tension in the Now*

The four elements which swirl around that centre are also concepts we have met before. With **purity of motive** we are driven by the emerging needs of the whole. Our narrow self-interest moves over and we are driven by the evolutionary impulse. **Natural hierarchy** is the idea of nested hierarchies or holarchies, where everything is a part and a whole, and where each new level transcends and includes the previous ones. **Integrity of Action** happens when we choose every moment to be free and whole and to express that in our actions. We walk our talk. Integrity of Action flows from us once we have aligned ourselves with the bigger context. It does not feel like an obligation to serve others or the planet. Rather, it is a joy to fulfil our highest potential. **Evolutionary Tension** is part of our continuing journey. No sooner have we reached a place of clarity than the next questions begin to emerge. We sit comfortably with this tension and open up to what it has to teach us about our next steps. This is what it looks like on the s-curve:

When these four elements are alive in us, we are aligned with the natural workings of the universe. We are an embodiment of evolutionary leadership, leading ourselves with the greatest integrity.

This can all seem very clear and fixed. Clarity is important, but at the same time there is a great mystery to it all. The work really begins when our soul starts to walk the path that our mind can see.

Story

Meanwhile, back at the CHE... It is the spring of 2006. I had tasked the Integral Organisation Development constellation to come up with a proposal for the structure of the CHE. When it arrived in my in-box, I felt my gut do a summersault: I knew that this was not a proposal I could accept. It was full of references to a community of equals, democratic leadership elections and suggestions that told me that this proposal had emerged from a post-modern centre of gravity. I knew what I had to do, but I didn't like it. I knew I had to take on my leadership role, thank the group for their work, but let them know that I couldn't accept their proposal. It pushed all sorts of buttons in my system – around fear of rejection, not being liked, and so on – and yet deep down I knew that if I did not draw a clear boundary now, the identity of the organisation would become vague and energy would seep away. The implications were that I had access to more complex value systems, and this would not go down well with the group, especially if they had a lot of post-modern Green. So keeping my heart as open and my mind as clear as I could, I wrote the note. It took a while to deal with the aftermath, during which I learned more about my Authentic Self than ever before. Some of the group stepped out of the organisation, others have gone on to play a key role. I know it was a defining moment for me as a leader and for the organisation.

SUMMARY

- We are the Ground of Being.

- When we recognise this, we feel our authentic selves emerge, as the spirit of the universe pulses through us.

- To achieve this breakthrough, we have inner work to do

CHAPTER FOUR

Looking After Ourselves

What's it gonna take to stay awake?

we wakin' up all the time
I'm wakin' up as I sit here and rhyme,
when i get lost in the flow of a river
feel a cold shiver
notice the clouds gather on a stormy day
feel sadness as one I love passes away
see a huge vista from a mountain top
and stop and bing!
my heart begins to sing
and I know I'm here for a reason
to ignore this inner voice is my treason
it's like trapping the year into one season
the winter of discontent
was not meant
to last a lifetime
so I rhyme
to keep me connected to my inner voice
the place from which I can make a clear choice
to live close to my passions and serve my happiness
I confess
that's my deepest need
to surrender and let my soul feed
cause if I am happy the world becomes a better place
cause I am the world
and the world is me

see
that sets me free of responsibility to anything other
that living a life I love
that fits me like a glove
set free the dove

time to park the ark
and play in the sand
bring on the brass band
to celebrate the living of our greatness
then feeling of being weightless
and buoyed by the spirit
of the universe
which is my spirit
which is everyone's spirit
cause nobody owns this vibe
we all coming from the same deep tribe
gotta stay connected
to the flashes of truth
before I shoot through the roof
My lifetime is at stake ...

what's it gonna take to stay awake?
to break
the consensus trance
take a stance then
dance the circle dance
with life and death
we linked to the earth by our body and breath
every 7 years our cells completely renewed
don't be confused
we all a part of the
great unfolding

great moulding
of the universe
we are the one
the rising of the sun
already begun
I'm refusin'
the illusion
sold to me on my TV
in school
who they tryin' fool?
I ain't buyin' in no more
I only shop store of core
where you can buy the best
of human potential
assessed
by universal principles of power
you can get
the weapons of the warrior for the fight
compassion and insight
plant the stake
set it alight
let the beacons burn from one mountain top to the other
the great soul is rising
the collective intelligence, the mother
bullshitters, duck for cover
make way
here comes the time of the mighty lover!

(by Tim Merry)

G iven an intention to be free and whole in the world, this chapter explores how we can support our inner state through the way we look after our physical organism – the body which houses us on this journey. It is a chapter I almost didn't write, and have struggled with more than the others. I didn't feel its total relevance, and couldn't find the right way in. I knew it was one of the quadrants and should therefore be included, but I am not a doctor or physician – and there are encyclopaedias of information about this out there.

It then became clear that the only way to approach this huge topic was through the story of my own journey, touching on the different elements that I have come across on my own path to greater fitness. Once again, the different explanations I give here are not meant to be the definitive authority on the particular topic – far from it (see Murphy (1994) for a great example of an integral approach to our organism). Rather, the whole chapter is once again designed to point to the way to how we can start thinking about our organism with this perspective of evolutionary fitness.

Fitness is about how the parts relate to the wholes and to each other. Given that everything is both a part and a whole (a holon), it is about how it all fits together. How are the different parts of my organism relating to each other and to my body as a whole? How am I relating to the context around me? Am I finding my connections, my fit-ness? How are we as human beings relating to our bigger context? Fitness all the way up and all the way down. Given that our subtler bodies must transcend and include our gross physical body, the relative fitness of our physical organism will influence the workings of our Mind and Soul.

The healthier the base, the more stable the higher structures. Developing evolutionary leadership in ourselves therefore requires that we pay attention to our body.

It used to puzzle me that Ken Wilber's description of the Upper Right quadrant included both "behaviour" and the physical organism. While I understood that they were both exterior expressions of the individual, the relationship wasn't clear to me. So I looked up "behaviour" in the dictionary and found the physiological definition: "response to stimulus". This connected it up for me.

What we normally call "behaviour" (people's conduct that we can see) is of course a response to stimulus: reactions to what is arising around us. This is also what our physical organism is about – responding to the different stimuli constantly bombarding it and keeping us running as efficiently as possible. This quadrant is therefore all about how we adapt and respond to the world around us, as a whole physical organism. Creating the conditions in our physical selves which will maximise our ability to respond to emerging needs is therefore a key part of leading ourselves from an evolutionary perspective.

Food

My first awakening to my body in this way was while I was living in Paris in 1992. For many years I had had skin problems, and the doctors had continually prescribed antibiotics and cream which seemed to dry up my skin. I'd been swallowing antibiotics daily for about eight years at this point (the thought still makes me shudder). At an alternative health fair, I came across a book called Food and Healing by Annemarie Colbin

(1986). It was my first initiation into the concept of supporting the body to look after itself, of seeing the body as a creative organism which much of the time just needs the space in which to harmonise itself, rather than external interference.

The book explained how dairy products are often one of the main causes of skin problems. I got very excited about this, seeing for the first time the possibility of reclaiming responsibility for my own body. I decided to take the plunge and cut out all dairy products. It was no small sacrifice, as I was currently working my way through the cheese stand at the local Parisian market. At the same time, I stopped using all the antibiotics and face ointments. It worked, and still works to this day. I occasionally consume dairy products to test whether I still react, and sometimes I just allow myself something nice although I know it contains dairy products. I usually pay the price, but at least it's a conscious choice and I know what I'm doing to my body. This was the big difference.

Colbin describes different approaches to food in her book, and suggests you select the one that feels best for you. I decided to go for the whole-food vegetarian option. According to Colbin, when you stop burdening your body with food that needs a lot of energy to process, your body starts to clean itself up. Around six months after changing your diet in this way, you are likely to get a major recurrence of any repetitive illnesses you have had in the past. Sure enough, after exactly six months, I got an intense sore throat. Following her advice, I tucked myself up in bed for a couple of days, drinking only ginger tea and vegetable broth, sweated it out, and it was over. I haven't had a major recurrence since.

These examples simply illustrate how, by paying more attention to our body, and seeing it as a creative, resilient organism, we can become more aligned with ourselves as a natural system. When we support our body to look after itself, it becomes increasingly evolutionarily fit, and energy is released which our organism can use to do all sorts of other exciting and interesting things – supporting us on our own higher evolutionary quest.

Acid-Alkaline

Kees Hoogendijk has inspired much of my thinking in this area too. He introduced me to a simple but profound way of checking on fitness. He was interested in the idea of acidity and had a sense that it somehow connected many of the areas he was working on related to health. In his explorations, he discovered that all the things we tend to think of as unhealthy trigger acidity in our bodies: caffeine, alcohol, nicotine, stress, electro-smog (e.g. radiation from mobile phones and computer screens). It seems that the longer the body is exposed to acidity, the more likely we are to be hit in one of our weaker spots, and to develop illness. Acidity creates decay, as we all know from those old school chemistry experiments. So if people are generally too acidic at the moment, it should be no surprise that our societies are decaying, and that we are creating an acidic environment with our pollution. Remember acid rain? Acid breaks things down.

Kees and I went on to explore what exactly acid and alkaline are – I had forgotten all my chemistry lessons! Water is made up of H_2O, which is a combination of hydrogen ions (H+) and hydroxyl ions (OH-). More H+ creates acidity, more OH- creates alkalinity. Hydrogen atoms normally have one proton in their nucleus and one electron spinning round it. When the number of electrons is either larger or smaller, the atom is called an ion. Hydrogen ions (H+) are missing an electron, and so have a positive charge. They are hungry atoms, looking for a new electron. They will eat up the electrons of other substances, hence acid's reputation for causing decay. Hydroxyl ions (OH-), on the other hand, have an extra electron and a negative charge, and are looking to give that electron away. When they get together, they form water (H_2O), which is the basis of our physical organism.

Here we find the yin-yang thread back again. Yin is like the sacrifice-self systems which seek to fit into the world, giving in order to connect, in this case like OH-. Yang is like the express-self systems which try to make the world fit to them, taking in order to feel whole, like H+. This would conform to our picture of a world in need of reconnection, a world too acidic, breaking down in decay. An important part of healing ourselves and our world, establishing that reconnection, is creating less acidity in ourselves.

H+ and OH- are complementary ions and we depend on both of them. If we swing too far into alkalinity we will stagnate. To measure acidity and alkalinity we use the pH scale, where a pH of 7 is neutral. A very easy way to test this is using litmus paper, where the colour of the paper indicates the relative acidity or alkalinity. Kees gives packs of litmus paper to people so they can test their current state by simply licking the paper. A saliva test gives you an idea of the state of the enzymes flowing through your body, the activity of the liver and stomach, and the effect on all the body systems and tissues. Ideally our pH level will stay between 6.5 and 7.5 all day.

Annemarie Colbin outlines the significance of this balance to our health. The pH of our blood plasma must remain at between 7.35 and 7.45. Any deviation either way creates problems. An acid pH in our blood plasma of 6.95 results in diabetic coma and death, while an alkaline pH of 7.7 causes tetanic convulsions and eventual death. We can see how the extreme acid-yang is offset by an extreme alkaline-yin (coma), and that the extreme alkaline-yin is offset by an extreme acid-yang (convulsions). The energies are in an intrinsic balance and any extreme swing either way will cause an extreme pull back in the other direction.

The body manages natural fluctuations. Interestingly, when our system produces acids, they are broken down into water and carbon dioxide, which are then expelled through the kidneys, skin and lungs, resulting in more acidity, more CO_2 emissions. Could this illustrate a possible link to us as the planet? Acidic societies creating too much CO_2, leading to global warming…

It is interesting to see that the natural pH level of our blood plasma is not neutral (pH 7), but slightly alkaline (pH 7.4). People often point to water as being neutral pH 7, but that is purified water. In nature, water is also slightly alkaline, like our blood plasma. It seems that life needs an imbalance to keep it moving. Tellingly, that imbalance in us inclines towards the alkaline, more OH-, which, remember, is looking to give away electrons: sacrifice-self for connection. Could this be related to our spiritual quest for a return to oneness or connection to our original source? Despite the continual dance of yin and yang, are we not ultimately more inclined towards connectedness and community? This was certainly what Howard Bloom unearthed in his exploration of living systems: living organisms are constantly seeking to evolve better ways of connecting in community.

The Earth, too, is negatively charged (yin), taking in surplus electrons from the Sun through the North Pole. The Sun is positively charged (yang). So as creatures of the Earth, it might make sense that we have a tendency towards the yin, towards order, towards love. Although this may not be uppermost in our awareness at this point in our history, when we talk to people about their deepest desires, wholeness and connection seem to be fundamentally shared dreams.

So the important question then arises of how we can avoid too much acidity in ourselves and keep a good balance. This is particularly challenging when the industrialised world around us is clearly more acidic than alkaline. As mentioned above, Kees found that caffeine, theine, alcohol, sugar, fats, nicotine, stress, and electro-smog all cause acidity. A first step would then logically be to avoid the things that we know trigger too much acidity. In the case of food and drink it is easy to see how to do this*.

When it comes to electro-smog, we can be conscious of our use of mobile phones, keeping them off where possible, and away from our bodies). There are also now products on the market that can help us to protect our electro-magnetic field from these influences.

In terms of stress, deep, regular breathing (as practiced in yoga) and meditation reduce acidity. So in this respect we can see a clear link to our practices for being an evolutionary leader in Chapter 3.

---

* You will find a useful table of acid and alkaline generating foods and drinks at http://www.soulhealer.com/ph.htm

Water

Water is a key part of this whole story. Our body is composed of around 70% water and our brain even more. We should therefore be interested in the properties of water if we are interested in our own health. The first important point is to make sure that we drink enough water. We should drink around two litres per day. Next comes an interesting question around the quality of that water.

A Japanese researcher, Dr. Masaru Emoto, has explored the nature of water crystals*. When water from a mountain stream is analysed, the crystal is beautifully ordered and a joy to behold. When inner-city water is analysed, the crystal is much more vague and not nearly as beautiful. If you take two glasses full of water and send positive thoughts to one and negative thoughts to the other, then the positive water crystals come out looking more like the mountain water, and the negative ones look more like the inner-city water. This of course has major implications, particularly when we remember that we are 70% water!

We can see this as a confirmation that thought and emotions influence matter. Consequently, if we send out positive or negative thoughts towards someone (including ourselves), we influence that person's physical wellbeing and therefore also their emotional state. We can of course also go at it the other way round, and be aware of the impact of the quality of water that we drink. If we drink ugly water, it is less likely to support an inner state of clarity and compassion. It is now possible to buy attachments for your taps that energise your water so that it comes out

---

* See www.hado.net.

in a healthy form. This is not purified water, but water that is run over minerals and the fundamental platonic forms and through a vortex to giving you lively, ordered and sparkling water. As such, it supports a higher order in us. Of course there are always many other impacts, but water is such a basic part of our make-up that it is worth being conscious consumers. A glass of energised water with a slice of alkalising lemon will do wonders to keep you well balanced!

Chakras

There is an interesting link between these different components of a healthy lifestyle and our chakras. Chakras are the energetic centres that connect us to the world around us, and act as drivers in our own development. Chakras plug us into the Universe. They are our keys to survival and evolution:

CHAKRA 1 connects us to where we're at, to the compound past of the present moment.

CHAKRA 2 awakens us to the Other and the bigger Holon, to unbounded creative, erotic, transcendental potential.

CHAKRA 3 crystallises our intent at that moment, creates our signature, forms our identity at the new level.

CHAKRA 4 opens us up to those around us, creates potential for connection.

CHAKRA 5 communicates our intent, what we have to offer, to those around us.

	CHAKRA	STIMULUS
7	crown	Meditation
6	third eye	Light and colour
5	throat	Music and sound
4	heart and lungs	Breathing
3	solar plexus	Natural foods
2	water and life energy (prana)	Energised water
1	earth, magnetism	Physical activity

TABLE 4.1: *The Chakras*

CHAKRA 6 provides us with insight to the next step of greater order and complexity.

CHAKRA 7 connects us to our more general evolutionary direction.

Each chakra can be stimulated by different activities and phenomena (Table 4.1, once again, with thanks to Kees Hoogendijk):

By exposing ourselves to the above stimuli, we can help keep our chakras spinning and tuned into the universe around us. We can also do so through visualisation, but if this is not supported by the way we treat our physical organism, it much less likely to succeed. One of Ken Wilber's key insights is that the lower sets the possibilities of the higher, so if we fail to look after our body, we limit the possibilities of our mind, soul and spirit.

In addition to diet, another essential aspect of looking after our physical organism is exercise. There is plenty of literature out there on this – you know what you could be doing!

Let us just clarify again why taking care of the body is such a core part of being an evolutionary leader. As we saw when looking at the acidity-alkalinity issue, the patterns within ourselves are fractals of the patterns in the world. To be as available as possible to the evolutionary process, we need to align our physical organism with its natural healthy state – which we notice is not one of pH 7 neutrality, slightly skewed towards connection. If we have our state right, there will always be healthy fluctuations within certain limits. We live in a changing world full of stimuli. Those stimuli impact on our physical organism, keeping it on its toes. Our job is to help keep our bodies resilient and adaptable, around a certain core state. In this way, we remain more open to the world around us and more able to respond healthily to the feedback and inputs we get. As Gandhi said, "we must be the change we want to see in the world".

In these busy times, we often fail to look after ourselves by neglecting to take the time to attend to our physical wellbeing – particularly if we are "busy" saving the world! Yet when we realise that we *are* the world, it makes no sense to try to fix the world without starting with ourselves. The current levels of stress in our society make it even more important that we look after ourselves. There are many ways to do this. The ideas above are food for thought, and meant to point towards a general approach to thinking about our bodies, rather than to prescribe specific methods. Go out and find the best way for you – just make sure that you do it!

SUMMARY

- Our bodies and behaviour are fundamentally intertwined with our inner world. If we look after our bodies we are likely to experience more inner development.

- There are simple things we can do to support our bodies to look after themselves. Drinking enough good-quality water is the first.

- Understanding how energy flows in our bodies is key to being able to look after ourselves.

CHAPTER FIVE

Experiencing Collective Evolutionary Leadership

The Rain

It's my own judgements that bring me down

The parting of the sea
Silver crowns adorn the ground
All around
Rain washes
My Bike cuts
A silver aisle
Soakin' wet I begin to smile

It's my own judgements that bring me down

Happiness
The never, never of never enough
Perfection
The constant internal correction
Voices in my head
Voting on my intention
Action and thinking
Punishments for Blinking
Punching holes in the hull
My ship is sinking

It's my own judgements that bring me down

My own sword
Is assured
To attack others with
The rigour
The vigour
That I apply to myself
Arising with stealth
The blade appears
Sharpened by fears
Cutting ones I love to tears
Seeing it in the light
The clouds part
The rain clears

It's my own judgements that bring me down

I wipe my glasses
Clearing off the wet
See the sunset
Lighting up the sky
Why
Didn't I see it before?
Too busy in darkness groping on the floor
For the light switch
Fumblin', mumblin', grumblin'
Rumblin' discontent
I know I was never meant
To feel this way
Then the rain woke me
Spoke to me

It's my own judgements that bring me down

How many times must I
Write the rhymes of the turning
I'm tired of burning
In my own witch hunt
Call the fire brigade bring on the clowns
Drop the frowns
The universe abounds
With rain
To wash away the pain
Again and again
Back to the heart
New start
But still messin'
With the same lesson

It's my own judgements that bring me down

(BY TIM MERRY)

What happens when a group of people come together who are all acting from a place beyond their separate sense of self, a place of deep connectedness, compassion and insight? Something very exciting!

Here we are exploring the lower left collective interior quadrant – the "We" (Webs of Culture). The intersubjective space, that exists between people in relationship. Relationship is not any of the individuals involved in the relationship. It is what lies between us. We feed it.

Our greatest ambitions to be free and whole are generally challenged most severely when we try engaging with other people. It's as if the universe is challenging us: "So you want to be free and whole? Well prove it! Deal with *this...*".

As we engage with others, we are confronted by the deepest parts of ourselves. The way we judge others is a projection of how we judge ourselves. After all, we are one. Me looking at you is the universe looking at itself. What I see is who we are.

Now when the ego is confronted by something it perceives as other or different, it is being called into relationship. This is not particularly appealing to our ego, as it is interested in its sense of separation, of uniqueness, of difference. And indeed, at one level we are all unique and exquisite individuals. We should not be denying that. But we are not *only* that. At a deeper level we are all profoundly connected. We go back 13.7 billion years together.

The ego likes to create boundaries between itself and the other, because to do so reinforces its sense of separation. "They are just different. It's all cultural. We just have to respect our differences, agree to disagree and move on. Hey, we don't want to suppress diversity, after all, do we? Well, if you really push me, then maybe we can compromise on something. I'll give up something if you give up something. Then we can safely maintain our distance, and we don't have to reveal our deeper selves – which might create some deep sense of relationship, horror of horrors!"

Going beyond our separate sense of self into deep relationship does not involve giving up any of our individual essence or integrity. In fact, *there must be no compromise.* We must trust that we can all be our highest and fullest selves and enter into relationship together. It requires a large degree of openness and willingness to engage in inner exploration. For as we sense resistance in ourselves to what someone else is showing of themselves, we have to dig deep, sense where that resistance is coming from and examine it closely. The resistance I feel is not about something that is "wrong" with the other. It is more about me. I am seeing part of myself mirrored in the other that I am not comfortable with, some mechanism that is helping me to maintain my sense of separation.

It may be that we sense a lack of integrity in the other. But that is no excuse to withdraw into our shell. Everyone has their own issues to deal with. In this case, our compassion is being challenged, along with our own integrity. If we can open our heart to the struggle that the other is having, it will help to transform it. This does not mean that we jump in and "rescue the poor victim". We can be with the other person and their suffering without getting pulled into it ourselves. If they feel love and understanding from us, as well as a trust that they are capable of dealing with it themselves, they will go away greatly strengthened and we will have done the best we can.

Learning to check with ourselves on the source of any discomfort we feel as we enter into relationship with others is an important part of evolutionary leadership. We feel compassion for ourselves and for the other as we become aware of our own dark corners whilst maintaining our connection to the ground of being and the deep knowing that nothing is fundamentally wrong.

There is a part of James Redfield's *Celestine Prophesy* that has remained with me. One of the core teachings is that in relationship, we should be drawing energy not from each other, but from a higher source. As separate individuals, our supplies of energy are limited. If a relationship is about shifting that limited energy between the partners, then it will be a roller-coaster ride of ups and downs that does not meet anyone's deepest needs. However, if we can draw energy from a higher, seemingly unlimited source, then "the pillars of the temple stand apart" (as Kahlil Gibran says in *The Prophet*). Apart, but deeply connected, holding a sacred space. Each partner is enhanced, as is the relationship itself.

When we manage to be together in this kind of space, great things can happen. When we transcend our sense of separation together, we connect. When we connect, something very tangible emerges between us. It is who "we" is. Like everything else, it transcends and includes the parts – us. Some form of collective being emerges. We feel as if we are swept up in a spiralling vortex of collective insight and compassion.

When we are in this space, an individual's voice becomes the voice of the collective. People channel what is there at the centre. What anyone says resonates with the rest. The conversation, or co-creation, builds like one whole. It is no longer a bunch of individuals with their own agendas or things they have to say in order to show how clever or important they are. It is a deeply interconnected conversation, which flows like one surging river with all sorts of streams feeding into it.

Each individual feels enhanced in the process, lifted up to their highest potential, contributing from the core of their being. There are no power games about whose voice is heard the most, for we speak as one. When I speak, it is impersonal. We all have our unique, sumptuous flavour to add, but it is drawn out of us by something greater. It is both surrender and upliftment in the same moment.

These are the spaces we need to create and nurture. As we move into a collective space beyond separation, we are tuning into the evolutionary flow of the whole itself. The universe flows through us, and speaks as us. We feel the way things truly are. We know intuitively what needs to happen. It is only in spaces such as these that we will develop enough collective compassion and insight to sustain us through the coming turbulence.

Most of my experience of this collective space has been in conversation circles (see Chapter 6 for details of how to host these). What excites me is the idea of a group of people *acting* together in that kind of space. When sitting in circle, we can see each other and the connection seems very tangible. But the connection is also immaterial, and should therefore persist whether we are sitting in circle or working on a project together – provided we can hold that same level of attention and consciousness.

I believe that this phenomenon of connectedness may be the same as what people call "flow" in the context of team sports. When we are playing a match, sometimes the team just seems to click. The passes flow perfectly, everyone is in the right place at the right time, each member of the team seems to know intuitively where the others are. It feels great, and is generally reported as being a peak performance.

It also reminds me of my theatre experience with Iranian director Saddredhin Zahed in Paris (who had worked with Peter Brook). When we rehearsed for a play, the text provided the basic framework, and the rest was done through improvisation. We also worked hard on our bodies and minds (only now do I really understand why). Working through improvisation is extremely challenging. I may get an idea and step into the space, but the space I step into is not empty. It also contains other people with other ideas, who are busy co-creating their story. The challenge is to find a way of offering what I have, whilst continually staying open to what the others are offering, and finding a way to blend them in a collective, creative whole that transcends and includes the parts.

Like the conversation circle, this type of group improvisation requires you to let go of your own agenda whilst maintaining your integrity and passion. If any of the individuals try to force their own idea onto the group, it breaks the whole co-creation process. It is the deep interplay of the yin and the yang. This was also the basis for our performances, for Zahed was determined that performances should not become fixed rituals where we just went through the motions every night without actually living the moment. We had a certain framework, but given that the details weren't fixed, we had to bring it to life every night. In order for that to succeed, all of the actors had to be "on form", i.e. open to a space of connection.

It was extremely challenging. More often than not we failed to create the kind of performance we strived for, but on the occasions when we did succeed, we knew it and felt it deeply – and the audience felt it too. Zahed called the troupe "Théâtre D-Nué", which means "naked theatre". Only now do I understand its deepest meaning. We had to be naked of our surface trappings and egoic interests in order to be truly able to co-create.

The task we face is to meet in collective space beyond separation, in all of our relationships with others. We live together in that space, we think together in that space, we work together in that space. At every moment, we have the choice. If we fail to do so, it is because we do not want enough to be free and whole. Engaging with people in a detached way means – far from being free and whole – being defined by the other. As Jean-Paul Sartre said in *Huis Clos*, "hell is other people". It doesn't have to be. Other people can also be heaven. It's up to us.

Story

Meanwhile, back at the CHE… It is the spring of 2007. For about a year now, we have been surfing a wave of high energy, busy out there in the world making connections. However, feedback is beginning to reach my ears that not everyone is happy with the way things are going. There is tension under the surface. At our May retreat we list all the projects that are going on and are amazed to see that there are nearly 50! No wonder we are feeling a bit stressed, particularly since we are still primarily a volunteer organisation. Another thing that comes to the surface is that relationships between people are strained and need attention. Essentially, we had been expressing our yang out there in the world, and were now being called back into our own yin energy of connection.

We called a meeting of all core people in the organisation (about 20 in total), facilitated by others in our network. The facilitators took us through a process of saying to each other things that we wanted to say and hadn't said yet (whether perceived as positive or negative). We became aware of the number of opinions we were forming of each other, and how those were acting as filters during our interactions. By naming those opinions, and checking with the other person if they recognised them or not, we made the implicit explicit and started to clean up our web of relationships. It released a lot of blocked energy. I also felt the collective energy settle down, as if roots had been sunk into the earth. As a result of this meeting, we could again see each other more clearly, have honest, grounded conversations connected to the reality of what existed and release ourselves from all the expectations we had of each other and the organisation. The foundations were being built from which we could go out into the world with greater centredness and focus.

SUMMARY

- The "we" resides in the space between us.

- We can nurture or pollute that space, depending on how we choose to relate to ourselves and the other.

- Seeing the other as a reflection of ourselves, as part of the whole, enables us to be more present and to act with greater compassion.

- A light and playful spirit helps us to avoid attachment and therefore to remain more available to the potential co-creativity.

CHAPTER SIX

Leading Evolution in our Systems and Structures

Feeling Strange

I fear not this feeling strange
it is the future being born
taking new form
the freshness of air after the storm

a slow rising
sense of arriving
letting go of striving
to get it all done
stopping now to enjoy the sun
feeling it has begun
when I slow
feel the speed trees grow
the way the rivers flow
there is an easier way
that feels like play
moulds me like clay
into what I am to become
bring on the rising of the sun
over the dark mountain range

I fear not this feeling strange
it is the future being born
taking new form
the freshness of air after the storm

the watered ground
the sound
of my heart explodin'
of the birds chirpin'
I want to ride the roads of this land like Dick Turpin
whoopin and hollerin'
into the unknown of tomorrow
into nameless joy and sorrow
and deeper learning
sitting in the burning
of our future unfolding all around
on watered ground

I fear not this feeling strange
it is the future being born
taking new form
the freshness of the air after the storm

(BY TIM MERRY)

The exciting question now arises: how do we create such collective spaces and processes in practice? As we design our organisations, the structures that support us in being together, what tools can help us create living, evolutionary systems?

This is Ken Wilber's lower right collective exterior quadrant. We have explored the inner state we need to cultivate (Chapter 3), how our physical organism can support it (Chapter 4), and the collective inner space we should nurture (Chapter 5). We have an idea of how life (evolutionary systems) works (Chapter 1) and our current situation (Chapter 2). Now it's time for collective design.

Don Beck calls it Natural Design, which means that it simply helps to support things the way they naturally are and develop. By connecting to our context from this perspective, we can align our systems and structures with the laws of the universe. This makes everything much less stressful and more efficient. We tune into the deep flow of the universal river, rather than trying to swim upstream, causing turbulence, stress and exhaustion as we go.

It is worth coming back to a few essentials here. We are seeking to support the basic evolutionary elements of autopoeisis (self organisation into wholeness – yang), adaptability (partness-yin) and transformation. In order to manifest this dance, an organisation must have enough order connecting the parts to hold it together as an organisation, while at the same time being open and flexible enough to constantly pick up and respond to feedback from its environment and the bigger context. Although this dance is itself what drives development, we can further facilitate evolution by tuning in to *what is emerging from the future.* We do this by using our more subtle senses. In this chapter we will explore how to do all three: self-organise, adapt and transform.

Starting where we are

Remember the s-curves (Figure 6.1):

A core principle of evolutionary leadership is to meet life as it is – to meet people and organisations where they are. Identifying where a system is situated on its journey along the S-curve is the essential first step. There are two main elements to identifying the starting point. One is: which Spiral systems are currently predominant? The other is: at what stage is the system in the S-curve life cycle?

We will focus on the second question for the moment, as this will determine the kind of change intervention to be made. When a system is in the vertical phase (in between periods of intense change), it needs conformity enforcement to support its wholeness, rather than diversity generation to unsettle it. It is crucial to get a sense of the stage a system is at in its growth, in order facilitate the most appropriate action at that moment. To use the Change States language, if an organisation is showing signs of Alpha Fit, i.e. it has reached a new space and everything is going smoothly, then there is no need to introduce a pro- gramme to facilitate new emergence. The system must first deal with its current existential issues before it has any surplus energy for moving on again. *The focus is on maintaining organisational wholeness and fitness.* At the same time, the system must be open to feedback that will enable it to learn and shift as gracefully as possible.

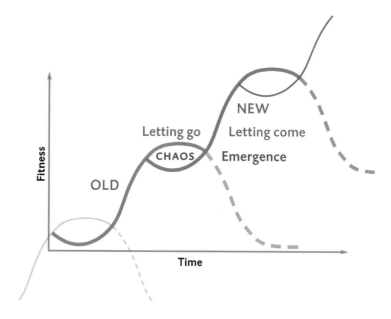

FIGURE 6.1: *S-Curves*

Here, other elements of Clare Graves' work, since adopted by Spiral Dynamics, can help to identify where an organisation is and what the most appropriate action is at that point. Graves identified a number of Change Conditions the presence of which determines what kind of change a system is ready for. Those conditions are:

1 There must be potential in the brain/brain syndicate.

The individual or collective must have the potential to move from their current place to a new place. If that capacity is not there, then there is no going anywhere. This potential can be identified by getting a sense of which Spiral systems are active and what kind of capacity for change is present. An example of the latter is whether people have a preference for first-order change (modifying current systems) or second-order change (shifting the whole system). Different "executive intelligences" can also be measured – looking at the spread of entrepreneurial, translational and transformational capacity. Entrepreneurial intelligence has the capacity to set up completely new systems, translational intelligence has the sense to maintain the good things from the current system, and transformational intelligence has the capacity to shift old systems into new ones. Measuring all of these factors, through assessments and interviews, gives a sense of the potential that is present.

2 Solutions must have been found to current and previous existential problems.

The issues which the current system emerged to deal with, as well as past issues, must have been solved before the system can fully move on to embrace something new. If there is still work to be done, then it is important to first complete it before moving on – otherwise there is unlikely to be a stable base on which the new system can stand free.

3 Dissonance must exist with the present system/condition.

There needs to be a sense of dissatisfaction with the status quo, in order to have the energy to push away from it and create the new. If the dissonance is not strong enough and the stress is not felt deeply enough, there is unlikely to be enough energy available to navigate a major change process.

4 There must be insight into probable causes of the problems and potential alternatives.

Once there is enough dissonance, there must be insight into what is causing the current problems that we want to solve, and some idea about how we could be doing it differently (even if this is not entirely clear yet). Seeing the causes is a relief, as we now know why things are the way they are. Sensing alternatives releases the energy to get on with experimenting with new ways.

5 Barriers to change must have been identified and overcome.

Once the causes have been identified, and energy released towards creating a more positive future, we need to identify and overcome the barriers that stand in the way. These may be inner, psychological barriers inside us or more structural, external barriers in the system. This requires moving into action.

6. Consolidation measures must be in place to support the change.

Often forgotten, this condition is essential for the long-term sustainability of any change. If one part of a system changes, but finds itself surrounded by expressions of the old system, it will have a real struggle to survive. So we need to build a supportive habitat for the new system to thrive in.

The presence or absence of these change conditions determines what kind of change can happen. The conditions map conveniently onto the Change States (Figure 6.2).

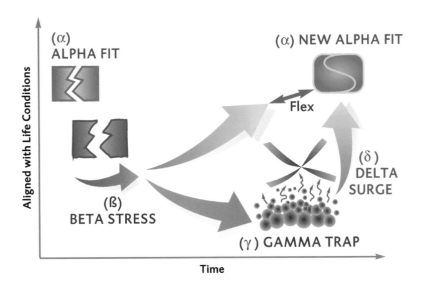

FIGURE 6.2: *Change States*

Potential and solutions (Conditions 1 and 2) refer to the stability of the old Alpha fit: is it a mature fitness which has served its original purpose? Dissonance (Condition 3) points to the stress that enters the system with the Beta and Gamma stages. Insight (Condition 4) suggests a move into a Flex or Delta stage. Barriers being overcome (Condition 5) would be a sign that we are moving to a new Alpha state. Consolidation (Condition 6) happens in the young new Alpha.

Graves identified eight different "Change Variations" – different types of change related to the stage that a system is in:

VARIATION 1: "Fine-tune or trim the tabs" (alpha)

VARIATION 2: "Reform or re-shuffle the deck" (alpha)

VARIATION 3: "Upgrade or improve on givens" (alpha)

VARIATION 4: "Down-stretch or regress to cope" (beta)

VARIATION 5: "Up-stretch or progress to deal" (beta)

VARIATION 6: "Break-out/Attack the barriers" (gamma)

VARIATION 7: "Up-shift/Morph to the next" (flex / delta)

VARIATION 8: "Quantum change of epoch proportions" (those rare quantum leaps in evolution)

The first five variations are first-order change (working on the current system), and the last three are second-order change (transforming into a new system). Fine-tuning (V1), reforming (V2) and upgrading (V3) are all appropriate at the Alpha phase when change conditions 1 and 2 are still being worked on. Down-stretching (V4) and up-stretching (V5) are appropriate in the Beta phase, when dissonance (condition 3) is already being felt. These involve reaching down to older systems to find stability, or reaching up to emerging systems to gather fresh insight. Break-out (V6) is specific to the Gamma trap stage. Upshift (V7) happens when there is also insight (condition 4) and the barriers (condition 5) are being engaged. Quantum change (V8) refers to a whole-system change where all elements are shifting at once to a new level.

All this points to the importance of identifying what kind of change is most appropriate for a specific context, based on where a system is in the journey through its life-cycle.

I identify two major strategies, which receive more or less emphasis based on where the system is. They are *designing fitness* and *facilitating emergence*. Designing fitness is appropriate for a system that is working on its Alpha fit, whether it is just entering a new Alpha, or maturing its current fitness. Facilitating emergence is appropriate for a system in a Beta or Gamma phase. Fitness and emergence are combined in the Flex and Delta stages.

Story

Meanwhile, back at the Corporation... our Change Agent has been made head of a business unit, and has asked me to help him try implementing all the theories we'd been talking about. We knew from the start that it was not a healthy unit – it had a poor reputation more widely in the organisation. One of the early interventions we made was to have employees take a Spiral Dynamics Integral CultureScan and then to interview them about the results. What was confirmed was a high level of dissonance with the current organisation and culture, with much Beta-Stress and a significant number of individuals in a Gamma-Crash phase. When linked to the value systems, we saw that most people experienced a Red power-driven environment, and desired an Orange performance-driven one. Here was our agenda for change.

Designing Fitness

We will start by looking at ways of designing fitness and wholeness in the organisation. Essentially, we are looking for *fitness across all four of Wilber's quadrants*, aligned behind a noble purpose that serves the world. One way of illustrating this would be in Figure 6.3.

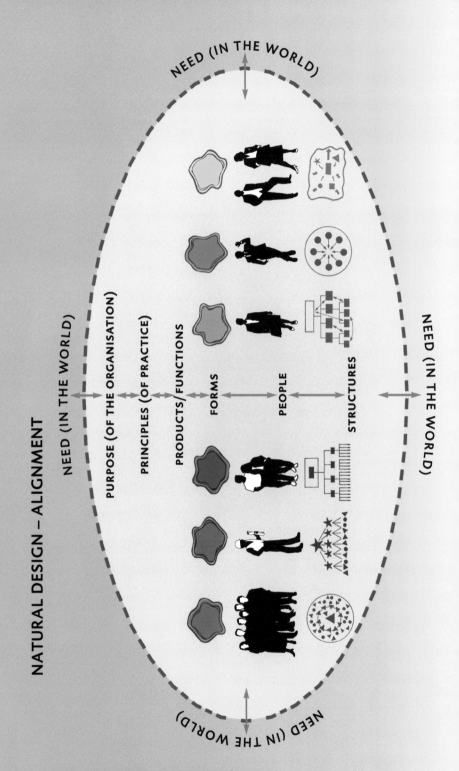

NATURAL DESIGN – ALIGNMENT

NEED (IN THE WORLD)

NEED (IN THE WORLD)

NEED (IN THE WORLD)

NEED (IN THE WORLD)

PURPOSE (OF THE ORGANISATION)

PRINCIPLES (OF PRACTICE)

PRODUCTS/FUNCTIONS

FORMS

PEOPLE

STRUCTURES

FIGURE 6.3: *Organisation by Natural Design*

The overarching element is *the need in the world* which the organisation aims to meet. With no clarity about that, the organisation is unlikely to survive. It is about its fitness with its environment. This identification with a need defines the Purpose of the organisation: it's reason for existence. The more its purpose resonates with a felt need in the world around it, the more energy the organisation will attract.

Holding the organisation together is a set of principles. These are guidelines for behaviour that, if followed, will enable the organisation to meet its purpose and the need in the world. They create coherence and congruence with the image projected to the outside world. The more an organisation embodies its principles, the more strongly it resonates outwards and attracts people to it.

In order to serve its purpose, the organisation needs to produce products and perform functions. While 'purpose' is the answer to Why? and 'principles' are the answer to a meta How?, 'products/functions' are an answer to What?

The next question is Who? Who should carry out these different functions? This is where the Spiral comes in, in the search for fitness between people, functions, culture and structures. Different functions will tend to fit more or less with the different Spiral Dynamics value systems. For example, a function requiring rigorous controlling, checking and recording (such as auditing) would resonate more with the Blue order-driven system. A function requiring dynamic experimentation, individual initiative and experiential learning (such as sales or advertising) would most likely resonate with the Orange success-driven system. A function requiring more human social skills and empathy (such as human resources or training) may well resonate more with the Green people-driven system. (Note that these are only examples, intended to suggest a way of thinking about fitness, rather than absolute truths.)

We align people with the functions that best suit them, based on the deeper Spiral codes. This is how to get motivated people: align their work with their deeper evolutionary needs. We then construct the habitats (systems and structures) around these people in their functions to reflect the different Spiral systems. A Blue department would look and feel very different to an Orange or Green department. The physical space would look different, the atmosphere would feel different, the motivational reward systems would be different, and so on.

Story

Meanwhile, back at the Corporation... we are in a management meeting, and I ask the team what are the main issues on their minds (I usually start meetings like this, without an agenda in advance). What surfaces is a tension felt by the two managers who lead the delivery part of the unit, i.e. the people who deliver the technology solutions to the client. The managers were sharing their frustration at really wanting their people to take more initiative, introducing them to the principles of self-directed teams, and yet constantly having their people come to them asking them what to do.

By now, the team was familiar with the value systems. I asked them which value system they thought would best support the functions that needed to be carried out in the delivery section. They agreed that the most supportive would be the Blue order-driven value system – they just needed to follow the agreed-upon processes efficiently. Then I asked them what kind of leadership would best match that value system. The coin started to drop. "So they actually need us to play a more authoritarian role, as that is what would best fit their value systems and help them do the work they need to do? So there's a mismatch between our value systems (Green consensus-driven wanting self-direction) and theirs...". It was an interesting moment. They realised that they had a choice – either to light-up their own Blue order-driven value system (which they both admitted having a little allergy to) or to find someone else to lead that unit who had a more natural fit. In the end, one of them stayed and one moved on.

Clearly, we do not want to abandon more traditional ways of aligning people with jobs, such as appropriate skills, experience and so on. We simply add the deeper human element. Wilber calls it having vertical and horizontal solidarity. Vertical solidarity reflects resonance with the Spiral systems. Horizontal solidarity reflects matching surface interests, skills, domains of practice and so on.

Natural design gives an organisation a clear identity to the outside world, combined with a healthy fitness inside, where people are working in environments which support them to be who they are, behind a clear purpose and guiding principles, for the good of the whole.

This fitness is a key factor in enabling the organisation to absorb shocks from the outside and self-organise in response. This is because when fitness is present, people's energy is not being squandered on struggling with systems and structures that go against their very nature. Rather, they have surplus energy for creativity and innovation, that they can channel into dealing with external shocks when they arise, at the same time as performing their normal function and keeping the system running.

The same is true for our bodies. When we are fit and well, we can absorb a certain amount of stress from outside without stopping our everyday activities, and we can respond creatively. Maintaining organisational fitness is the way to insure that the organisation can respond to the call for more intense change when it comes.

To understand what this might involve in practice, we can look at another aspect of Ken Wilber's thinking. He sees reality as being composed of "holons", a term coined by Arthur Koestler to denote something that is both a part and a whole. So everything is both a whole in its own right and part of something bigger. Wilber identifies holons as having four main capacities:

- "Agency", the capacity to clarify identity, wholeness and boundaries, and express this in the world.

- "Communion", the capacity to connect to whatever is outside those boundaries.

- "Self-transcendence", the capacity to go beyond one's current stage on the evolutionary path.

- "Self-immanence", the capacity to hold all one's parts and past together in the present, healing and integrating past patterns.

When designing fitness, we focus on the capacities for agency and communion. Self-transcendence and self-immanence come into play when we start facilitating emergence. These four capacities all play out in the individual and collective arenas. The table in Figure 6.4 illustrates how this theory can be applied to designing fitness in organisational development (with thanks to Diederick Janse for his co-creation).

FOCUS IN HOLON	MANIFESTS AS...	HOW?	INDICATOR	EVALUATION METHOD E.G.
Individual tran-scendence	personal U-process, vision quest	personal coaching	how well the energy of change is flowing	Spiral assessments plus interviews
Collective tran-scendence	collective U-process, chaordic emergence	team coaching	how well the energy of change is flowing	Change dynamics assessment
Individual self-immanence	healing and integrating past patterns	individual therapy	how influenced you currently are by past patterns	Spiral assessment ; therapy
Collective self-immanence	healing and integrating past patterns	Organis-ational constellations work	how influenced you currently are by past patterns	Organisational constellation (Bert Hellinger's work)

TABLE 6.2: *Capacities for Agency and Communion*

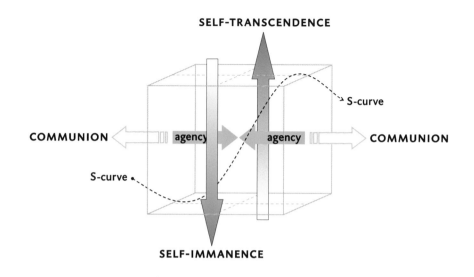

FIGURE 6.5: *Capacities in a Living System*

Facilitating emergence

The natural fitness design described above is the ideal state or an organisation to be in. However, as we know, the world is evolving and all the elements of this design are continually shifting and changing. Sometimes larger-scale changes, either inside or outside a system, call for a more substantial, second-order change. Given our current global context, which we could describe as a well-developed Beta stage, if not Gamma, there is currently a widespread need for second-order change, triggered primarily by our rapidly-changing life conditions and the shifts in people's consciousness. In order to meet this need, a deeper process of transformational change is needed, that will bring us to a new level of fitness. This section describes ways of approaching that process.

GOAL IN HOLON	MANIFESTS AS...	HOW?	INDICATOR	EVALUATION METHOD EG
INDIVIDUAL AGENCY	uncovering an individual's purpose	personal coaching	how clear someone is on their own purpose	interview
COLLECTIVE AGENCY	uncovering underlying codes, rules and patterns	chaordic design analysis	level of internal organisational fitness	Spiral Dynamics CultureScan; interviews
INDIVIDUAL COMMUNION	interpersonal & communication skills (Spiral)	EQ; personal coaching	how well others receive your communication	360 degree evaluation
COLLECTIVE COMMUNION	feedback and response loops	systemic design	quality of your interaction with others	customer satisfaction / supplier reviews;

TABLE 6.3: *Designing Fitness*

Before moving onto the details of the processes we can use, it is worth taking a closer look at what we are doing when we facilitate emergence, to see the processes in their context. To do this requires an understanding of what Ken Wilber calls States and Stages.

States and Stages

We have already encountered the notion of stages in the Spiral Dynamics Integral model. Transformational facilitation processes can be applied at any stage on the Spiral. This is because they are related to permanent states that we always have access to*.

Ken Wilber talks about three universal states accessible to people at all levels of development: waking, sleeping and deep sleep. In our waking state, there is a world that we are aware of. We can see it and talk about it. However, in order to be able to see the world in its wholeness and make sense of it, we need a place from which to look, which must by its nature be more complex than the world that we see. So we have a lens, which makes sense of the world for us. When we are in the waking state, we cannot be aware of that lens, because it is our waking awareness itself – in the same way that a fish, immersed in water, is not aware of its wider context.

However, we access that place of awareness whenever we enter the dreaming state. It is important to note that we do not have

---

* The States described here are a different category than the Change States described above.

to be asleep to enter a dreaming state: it is a shift of consciousness that can be achieved while we are awake. What we are accessing in this state is our awareness itself, which, because it transcends and includes our waking world, contains all the relationships between the waking parts and can therefore, by its nature, hold more complexity.

There is also another state we can access. Our sense of awareness itself has emerged from a bigger context. Our dreams emerge out of this deeper ground which lies beyond the dream state: the state of deep sleep. When in deep sleep, we do not dream. Instead, we are plunged into the formless ground out of which our dreaming emerges. Again, it is possible to access the deep sleep state when we are awake, through meditative practice and by quieting ourselves to tune into that source.

To sum up, we have the waking state, the dream state and the deep sleep state, each one being respectively more complex than the last, as the dream state transcends and includes the waking world and the deep sleep state transcends and includes our dream world.

Our different Stages of consciousness flow through these states. So, to take the Spiral Dynamics levels as an example, we may see Green (and below) in our waking world, with Yellow as our dream state awareness, and Turquoise as the deep sleep ground. Another way of expressing the relationship between these states would be Transcended (waking), Proximate (dreaming) and Emerging (deep sleep). What makes up our waking world is that which we have transcended, what makes up our dream world is the very lens through which we are currently looking at the world, and what makes up our deep sleep world is the stage that is emerging into our consciousness.

STATE	Emerging	Proximate	Transcended
WORLD	Deep sleep	Dreaming	Waking
FORM	Causal	Subtle	Gross

TABLE 6.1: *States of Consciousness*

These states can therefore be said to have different forms. That which we have transcended and which exists in our waking world has gross form: we can see it with our physical eyes. Our awareness in our proximate state has a more subtle form (it cannot be touched, we can connect to it only with our subtle senses). And it all seems to emerge out of this vaster ground in deep sleep, which we therefore call "causal": that which brings the subtle and the gross into being. The stages flow, then, from emergent causal into proximate subtle to transcended gross.

Why is this important? Because when we are facilitating emergence, the stage that is preparing to manifest in the gross, waking world is already present in the subtle, dreaming world. Similarly, the space where we can be conscious of that subtle, dreaming world is in the causal deep sleep world. If we can become conscious of the subtle plane by shifting our awareness into the causal plane, then we can start more consciously helping our future to manifest. So doing, we speed up evolution, bringing the potential into the real more swiftly. And because everyone spends time awake, dreaming and in deep sleep, everyone, whatever stage they are at, has access to these three states. I believe that our capacity to access them consciously and intentionally increases as we develop, but they are always part of everyone's life. The processes outlined help us become more conscious of our emerging futures.

Claus Otto Scharmer identified this bigger concept during the research that led to his definition of the U-learning curve. He was looking to see what it was about the most successful people in organisations that made them so successful. The essential factor turned out to be becoming present to the emerging future. His U-process looks like Figure 6.8.

At the Downloading phase, we are repeating our old way of doing things. As we shift to Seeing, we start to think about what we are doing, and become more conscious of it. We can look more closely at our behaviour and become aware of the details. Moving down to Sensing, we tune into our subtle state, to get a sense of what all those past behaviours feel like as a whole. Next, we deepen to Presencing, which involves a simultaneous letting go of the old gross whole, connecting to what is present in the subtle by entering the Emerging state, and a *letting come* as the subtle is welcomed into the gross. This transition has to happen in a quality space, stimulated by asking deep questions such as "Who is my Self?" and "What is my Work?" Such questions tap into the stage that is present in the causal form – our greater, emerging selves.

At this point, having journeyed from the old gross world into its subtle context, and connected to what is emerging in the causal, we can then consciously shift the stage that is in the causal state into the subtle state, "crystallising from the future field". What does it feel like there? How would it feel to be/live/work like that? The next stage, Prototyping, helps us to see the new system in our mind's eye. What does it look like? How can we conceptualise it? Those ideas are then enacted, bringing them from the subtle dream world into the gross waking world, with Realising – the concrete practice. After a while, of course, it starts all over again…These states also relate to the stages in the S-curve we saw in Chapter 1 (Figure 6.7).

STAGES IN EVOLUTIONARY SYSTEMS

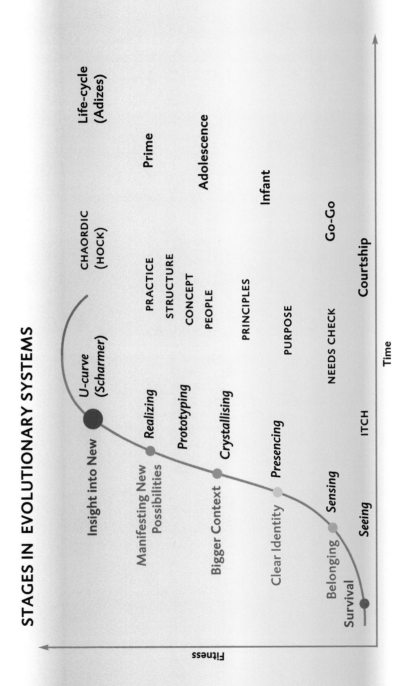

FIGURE 6.7: *Stages in the S-Curve*

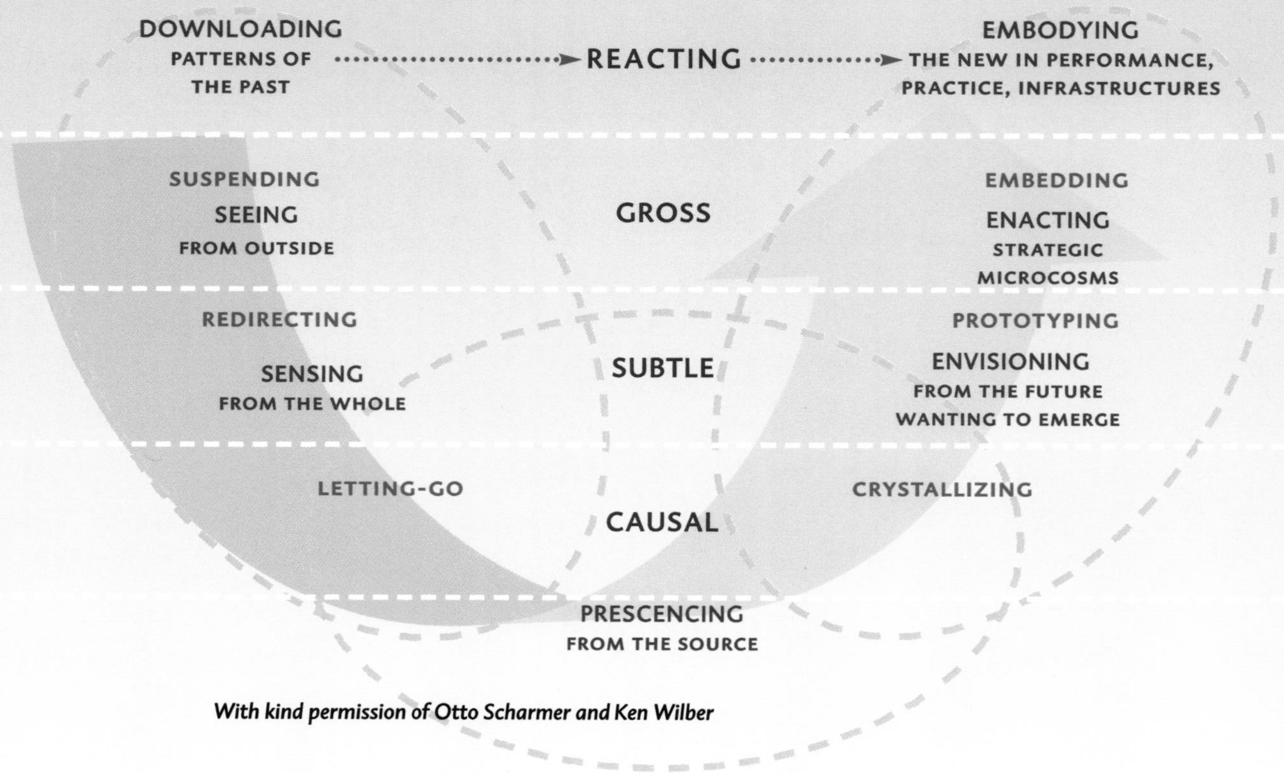

FIGURE 6.8: *Otto Scharmer's U Process*

DOWNLOADING
PATTERNS OF
THE PAST

REACTING

EMBODYING
THE NEW IN PERFORMANCE,
PRACTICE, INFRASTRUCTURES

SUSPENDING
SEEING
FROM OUTSIDE

GROSS

EMBEDDING
ENACTING
STRATEGIC
MICROCOSMS

REDIRECTING
SENSING
FROM THE WHOLE

SUBTLE

PROTOTYPING
ENVISIONING
FROM THE FUTURE
WANTING TO EMERGE

LETTING-GO

CAUSAL

CRYSTALLIZING

PRESCENCING
FROM THE SOURCE

With kind permission of Otto Scharmer and Ken Wilber

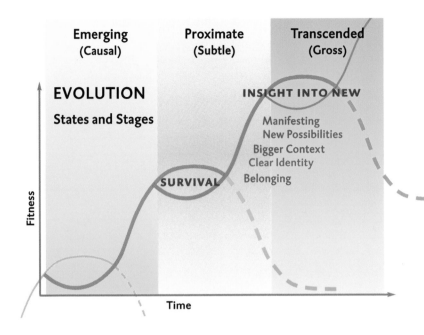

FIGURE 6.9: *S-Curve and States of Consciousness*

In the critical phase of chaos, we can access the emerging future system by connecting to our causal and subtle states. The stages of *survival* and *belonging* are still connected to the old system that we are transcending. The stages of *clear identity* and *bigger context* become our new proximate state, the way we see and manifest as the world. The stages of *manifesting new possibilities* and *new insight* are our higher potential.

Facilitating emergence thus calls for a design flow that will help to make explicit in the waking world what is already implicit in our dream world. Here is a synthesis of the different models we have looked at so far in Figure 6.7.

There are two possible scenarios for facilitating emergence. The first involves a context where a small number of people from a larger organisation or system gather to explore the need they are sensing for a new way of being. None of them are in positions of responsibility from which they can change the structures through their own authority and power. We will call this the "Imaginal Cells Scenario". Imaginal Cells is the name given by evolutionary biologists to the cells of the butterfly that begin to emerge as the caterpillar dissolves in the cocoon.

The second scenario involves an individual or a group of people who occupy a position of responsibility in their organisation or system from which they can initiate a whole-systems change involving people who work "under" them. This we will call the "Conscious Design Scenario".

In the Imaginal Cells Scenario, the focus is purely on facilitating emergence as described in the first section below. There are no structural interventions, as we are assuming that the people involved do not have the power to authorise them. However, once the Imaginal Cells start to take off and resonate more widely in the organisation, people in higher places are likely to notice and initiate more Conscious Design initiatives.

John Stewart, in *Evolution's Arrow* (2000), points out that there are two major ways in which living systems protect the collective space from the self-interest of the parts. One he calls Internal Management, and the other External Management. In Internal Management, all the parts of the system agree on certain behavioural norms and self-regulate for the good of the whole. In External Management, an outside factor regulates the system, ensuring that the parts do not take a free ride on each other's co-operation in their own interest, but only act for the good of the whole.

The Imaginal Cells scenario works primarily on facilitating the conditions for Internal Management, whereas the Conscious Design scenario includes more elements of External Management as well.

The Imaginal Cells Scenario

In the process described below, I have connected the Chaordic design flow with the U-process, as these are the approaches I am most familiar with and have experience of using in practice. They are not necessarily how Dee Hock and Otto Scharmer originally intended them to be used. This scenario reflects how working with these processes has helped me make sense of the dynamics at play and design emergent change processes. Officially, Dee Hock's process starts with 'purpose'. I have added two prior stages and have also given a specific focus of Communities of Practice to the 'structure' and 'practice' stages.

The stages of emergence include:

1 The Itch

A number of people in a collective system become present to a need. They feel dissonance with the old way of doing things and have some insight into how things could be done differently. They feel an itch to change. This would relate to Scharmer's Seeing stage: stepping out of the old system and seeing it from a distance.

2 Needs check

At this point, it is important to check what the need is, and how widely it is felt. If it is felt only in a few individuals, then this is unlikely to be the right moment for the organisation to engage in a whole-scale exploration of what is emerging. It may just be that individuals have issues of their own to address. If the rest of the organisation is doing fine and the individuals with the itch are stressed by the organisational context, then the best thing might be for them to go elsewhere and find a more supportive context: a better fit.

This does not mean that the system should ignore the feedback. A wise evolutionary leader will note it and keep an eye on its further development, whilst also reflecting on what it tells the organisation about its context and potential future. However, if the pre-sensing exercise uncovers a wider need in the collective, then we should move on to the next step, exploring the need more deeply and then acting on it.

Within the initial imaginal cell of change agents, we explore the need that they are sensing. Are they all seeing the same thing? What are the collective patterns that underlie what they see individually?

This exploration involves both Scharmer's Seeing the System phase and starting to Sense from the Whole – checking in with how people experience the system as it is.

3 Remembering Ourselves as Co-Creators

This is a key moment. So far, people have been pointing the finger critically at the system they are unhappy about – seeing the system out there. This has been an important first step, as it has allowed people to put some distance between themselves and the system, enabling them not to get caught up in its dynamics.

Now it is time to move on. People are themselves part of the system which they are pushing away from, and they are co-creating the very thing they want to change. It is essential that they acknowledge this. Once people begin to think about the ways in which they are maintaining the current system through their own behaviour, their relationship to it changes. The mentality shifts from "us versus them", to one in which I take responsibility for my own actions and lead by example. It also releases more compassion towards the old system.

This phase connects to "Sensing from the Whole" on the U-process. There is more heart energy here than in the earlier stages, where the head energy predominated.

4 Chaordic design

At this stage we start consciously co-creating the new system. Sensing our own connection and responsibility starts a process of letting go of the old, which creates space for the new to emerge. It starts with *purpose* and *principles*. In order to create a core purpose and principles, we must gather together the people who have become present to the emerging need, who are feeling the itch. They are the ones who can start to create the emergent system – the base line of the second S-curve. This must happen while the old system is still dominant and running the show (the top of the old S-curve), as everything needs to keep working while the new system develops. This of course creates tension. It is essential that the new system should have backing from someone high enough up in the organisation to be able to protect the boundaries of the space created for it emerge in. Otherwise it will just get squashed. Having high-level support does not mean that everyone in the organisation has to know what is going on – far from it. It is useful to stay "below the radar" until the new system is strong enough to start emerging in its own right. By that time it should be able to transcend and include the old system in a way that honours the traditional way of doing things, embracing the good parts and jettisoning the parts that are no longer useful.

Creating new purpose and principles happens in quality conversation space. These conversations create the container in which the change agents can connect, discover their collective patterns and clarify exactly what they are sensing. These conversations take place in Scharmer's Presencing and Crystallising steps. I will say more about the nature of these conversations below.

Next we turn our attention to the *people*. Given the new purpose and principles, who are the people who will in some way be connected to this enterprise? This includes all stakeholders, anyone with whom the system is going to interact, both inside and outside.

With an initial idea of the first three stages (purpose, principles and people), we start to explore the *concept*: what might the organising look and feel like? This is not yet about detailed structure, but rather about a *sense* of the system. What would it feel like to work there? What kind of organisation would it be? How might it be organised, in general terms? Are there any existing examples to draw inspiration from, or do we need to create something completely new?

Only after we have developed a concept do we move onto *structure*. Mindful of our purpose, principles, people and concept, what structure do we need to create? What systems will best support our purpose, principles and people? The structure exists to serve, not to be served.

At each new stage, we revisit the previous ones to check for consistency and congruence. Then we step into the practice.

5 Developing a Community of Practice

Once a container has been built for the people sensing the new need, that container must be developed into a space where these people can do the work they feel they need to do in order to contribute to the shift, and can safely exchange experiences and get support from each other. The core quality of an Imaginal Cell is that *the people in it practice being the way they would like the rest of the organisation to be.* It is not so much about starting up new initiatives (most of these Diversity Generators are busy enough anyway), but about transforming one's everyday practice. This is a community of practice, which would have both real-time supportive spaces and its own virtual environment.

This stage relates to Scharmer's prototyping and realising – exploring together what this new way of being is, trying it out and learning from each other's experiences.

Story

Meanwhile, back at the Corporation... you may remember that the first thing our Change Agent did, before he got the job at the business unit, was to initiate a change community. After our first conversation, he secured a small budget from his boss to take a group of people through an innovation process to improve the organisational culture. We planned six sessions, and they were related to the steps above.

After going through a first iteration of the Imaginal Cell formation, this group became a community of practice that met roughly every month to see how they could take the practice of their principles into their work in the organisation. The first draft of principles included:

- If you communicate something to a group, do so with respect for the individual.

- Communicate from a positive starting point.

- Listen with attention to the intention behind what people are saying.

- Dare to communicate.

- Dare to create the opportunities to listen.

- Act on feedback.

- Say what you're doing, and do what you say.

Out of this initial community, a number of projects emerged. They included other change communities, cultural change processes for business units, talks to all six hundred managers about this approach, and a central unit for cultural transformation. At the same time, the participants were simply trying to live the principles in their daily work, and were reporting back on their experiences of doing that.

What follows is more detail on how to facilitate each of these steps. I should say at this point that I do not intend to give a comprehensive guide of how to work with all the methods I mention. I will attempt to give you the essence of each method, and a sense of how each fits the flow we are working with. You can find out more about the details of the methods from the references. These are of course not the only methods you can use in these contexts. They are simply the ones that have worked for us so far. They serve to illustrate ways of thinking about the process at each stage of emergence.

When reading the following section, please bear in mind that it is not a step-by-step text book on how to facilitate emergence. The descriptions below draw on our experience at the organisation I co-founded, Engage!, of using these different methods in certain contexts. While the methods themselves are useful tools for this work, they do not occupy any fixed place in the flow described below. Ultimately, it is up to you to develop and discover these or other methods that can best serve your approach to this work. The last thing we want is for this to become a rigid gospel! Anyway, by the time you read this, our practice will also have moved on. The main point is that it is possible to work in our organisations using the principles of evolutionary leadership outlined above. This is the story of how we have experienced that work.

Facilitating the Itch

Normally, the itch develops by itself, as people within the system grow dissatisfied with the old ways and sense new possibilities. The main role for an evolutionary leader is therefore to identify the signs of itching. It is important for organisations to have feedback channels and spaces for the expression of dissonance arising in the system. This could involve a system of mentoring and coaching, where the mentors are able to feed back any signals they pick up which are related to the organisation and not just to the individual. Such channels could involve real or virtual "graffiti walls", where people who have an idea or want to express their dissatisfaction can do so immediately. There are many ways to stimulate feedback if one really wants to.

Most importantly, nurturing feedback should be part of the organisational culture. Those who have more decision-making responsibility should always be on the look out for it, and those who have feedback to give should know that it will be listened to and valued. We need to value feedback and disturbance as essential clues to the changing world within which the system finds itself, so that it can adapt more rapidly and survive more successfully in its context. This relates to the core evolutionary principle of adaptability.

Facilitating the Needs Check

The purpose of the needs check is to find out whether there is a widely-felt collective itch in an organisation (remembering that "organisation" can mean a collective system of any kind). Ways of facilitating this can range from one-on-one interviews to larger group gatherings. We have tended to work with the latter, following the principle that whichever people come to the meetings are the right people.

A key part of preparing for a gathering is the invitation. Remember that the point of the exercise is to determine whether other people are feeling the same Itch that the original Itchers identified. It is therefore vital to co-create the invitation with the original Itchers, helping them to articulate their feeling as clearly as possible. A good way to do this is to ask the group "what question would really get this organisation buzzing?", and to make that question the main focus of the invitation. "This is what we are going to explore at this gathering. If it touches you, then come along." If the invitation is a powerful expression of the Itch that people are feeling, then the number of people who turn up to the gathering will give you an initial idea of how widespread the Itch is. Remember that others may well be feeling it too, but are not ready to admit it.

At this point, I would like to offer a few words on the power of a good question. Questions play a central role in all the processes we are employing here. A good question taps into a learning edge for a group – shines the spotlight on an apparent polarity or dilemma that people are struggling with. It names various parts that have not yet been reconciled into a greater whole. In doing so, it invites more complex thinking and energy to work on transcending the dilemma and integrating the disparate parts – to create greater order. So a well-crafted question will stimulate the natural evolutionary process to transcend and include in greater complexity and order.

This was illustrated to me recently most graphically when someone told me about the new science of crystal energy. Crystals have by their nature a very ordered structure. Scientists have been experimenting with disordering the crystal's structure, holding the parts apart. The drive of nature is to create greater order, and the scientists have found that energy comes in to try and re-order the crystals. So holding the crystals apart generates energy. The same is true of a good question. In naming an unresolved polarity, we invite in the natural energy of the universe to transcend and include the parts in greater order. Asking the right questions at the right moment is an art which plays a major role in evolutionary leadership.

There are a number of ways you can facilitate gatherings for the Needs Check phase. As I mentioned earlier, it is important to have high-level support for the initiative inside the organisation, and that support must be clear at the start of the event. The high-level sponsor should be invited to say some words of support to open proceedings before handing over to whoever is facilitating, even if they don't stay for the whole event. One or more of the original Itchers should also speak, expressing as clearly as possible the Itch they feel, and why they have taken this initiative.

At this point, it is appropriate to go back to Chapter 5 on "We", and remember the quality of space we are seeking to create in relationships between people. A space where people leave their personal agendas behind, transcend their egoic sense of separation and connect to the good of the whole. Here we connect to the Subtle fields – Scharmer's Sensing. The Needs Check meeting is the time to create such a space – where people can speak from the heart and collectively sense the whole.

Facilitating Remembering Ourselves as Co-Creators

This is a sensitive moment in the group, as we drop down into the heart energy and the subtle fields. It is important to give people enough time to get their criticism of the existing system off their chests, so that they now have enough space inside themselves to open up to this new depth.

The core of this step is to remember that we are co-responsible for the world that we experience around us. We are literally co-creators, as all four of Wilber's quadrants co-arise simultaneously. We have been co-creating together since the moment of the Big Bang. However, we easily forget.

Having spent a while naming all the problems with the current system, and pointing at it "out there", it is time for us to take responsibility for the fact that we are co-creating it. At least some of our own behaviour is maintaining the current system. We have taken on many of the characteristics of the organisational culture, quite simply in order to survive in the current environment. There is no need to feel guilty about that. But we must reclaim responsibility.

You can ask people to name some of the characteristics they think they have adopted that do not really feel true to their deepest nature, and how they express these in their behaviour. What are you currently doing that is maintaining and contributing to the status quo?

It is also beneficial to give people "homework" to do between gatherings: have them notice a moment when their actions have been more strongly defined by the system than by their own integrity. Then invite people to bring their stories back to feed into the next meeting.

Facilitating Chaordic Design

At this point in the process, we start to design the container that will hold our new way of organising ourselves and being together. In order to do so, we shift into Scharmer's Presencing phase, to explore the deeper calling that we are sensing in ourselves and in the world, and where the two meet. To do this, we can also draw on the work of Dee Hock and his Chaordic process.

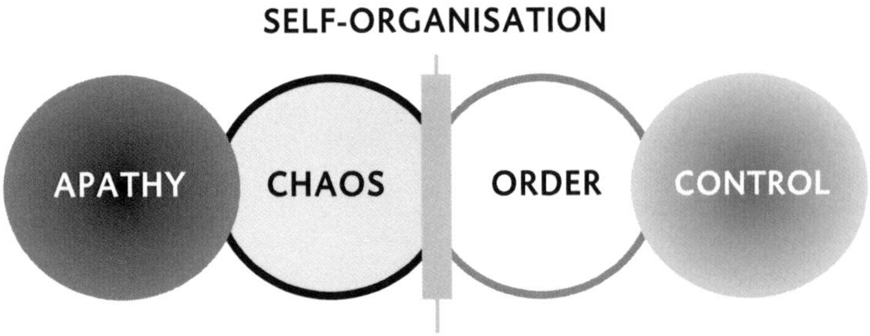

SELF-ORGANISATION

FIGURE 6.10: *Dee Hock's Operating Positions*

Dee Hock was the founder and CEO of Visa International. He created a hugely successful organisation and after doing so began to ask himself how he had done it. In that exploration, he discovered living systems theory (Figure 6.10) and saw the similarities in his approach, the primary one being the need for order and wholeness on the one hand and openness to chaos and adaptability on the other. Chaordic organisations need enough order to hold everything together, so that the ongoing response to the chaos of our emerging world can be channelled into a collective purpose supported by collective principles, creating transformation. When these conditions came together, the system seemed to self-organise (as natural living systems do). People just did what needed to be done in order to pursue the purpose in line with the principles. The yin-yang just danced its dance. Trying to control everything in top-down structures stifled life and emergence, and he had found a way of letting life in.

Many traditional organisations still attempt to operate in the space between order and control, not allowing in the chaos. When people at the top of an organisation over-control, this triggers apathy in those lower down the hierarchy, who are not given any responsibility to act and fulfil their potential. Likewise,

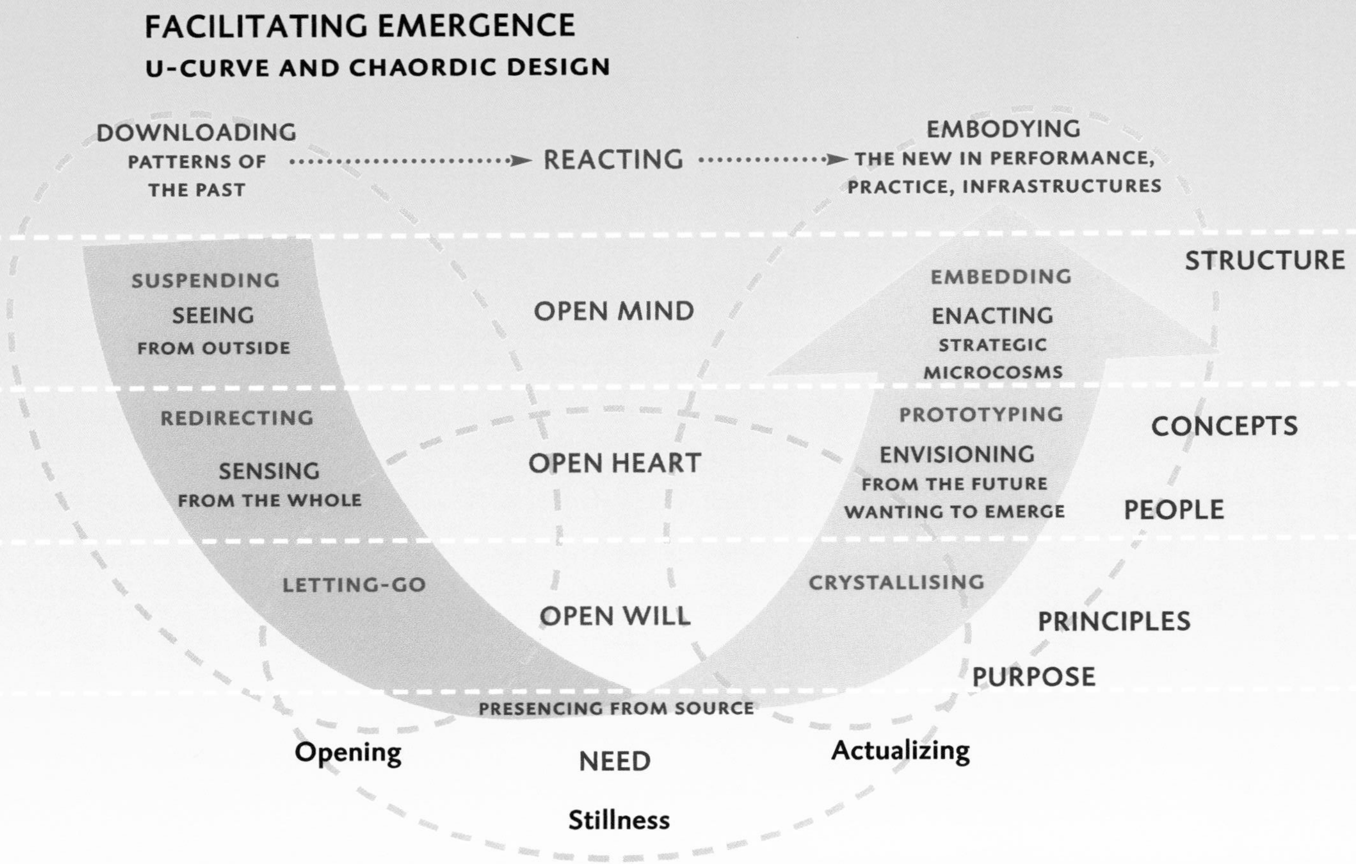

FACILITATING EMERGENCE
U-CURVE AND CHAORDIC DESIGN

DOWNLOADING .... REACTING .... EMBODYING

patterns of the past → the new in performance, practice, infrastructures

STRUCTURE

CONCEPTS

PEOPLE

PRINCIPLES

PURPOSE

EMBEDDING

ENACTING
STRATEGIC MICROCOSMS

PROTOTYPING

ENVISIONING
FROM THE FUTURE WANTING TO EMERGE

CRYSTALLISING

OPEN MIND

OPEN HEART

OPEN WILL

PRESENCING FROM SOURCE

SUSPENDING
SEEING
FROM OUTSIDE

REDIRECTING
SENSING
FROM THE WHOLE

LETTING-GO

Actualizing

NEED

Stillness

Opening

FIGURE 6.11: *U-Process and Chaordic Design*

when there is too much apathy in an organisation, it invites someone to step in and take control. Too much apathy leads to loss of identity (yin dominates yang). Too much control leads to loss of adaptability (yang dominates yin). It is the natural dynamic balance.

Organisations can function in a Control-Apathy way – in fact many do. But this way of organising is no longer adequate to the world arising around us. We need to be open to the feedback we are receiving from our context or we will not make it through the coming years. And given the exponentially increasing rate of change, who would want to be at the top of a command-control organisation trying to plan for the next five years and taking responsibility for all decisions? It's no wonder that so many top managers suffer from burnout and serious physical illnesses – they are going against the deeper flow, and if they persist it will literally kill them. Moreover, they may well take many of us down with them.

We have reached the stage where we must create containers for our work that are congruent with how we know the universe works. This means creating enough order to hold the whole together and give it direction whilst staying open to the emerging world and responding where needed. The Chaordic structure seems to be one way of doing this.

There are six main steps in the Chaordic process: Core Purpose, Core Principles, People, Concept, Structure, Practice. The steps map onto Scharmer's U-process as in Figure 6.11.

Our first step is to host meaningful conversations to elicit purpose and principles. We tend to do this in circle space. We also use interactive theatre processes – it depends on the group you are working with as to your choice of method.

Purpose

Dee Hock defines Core Purpose as "a clear unambiguous statement of that which we jointly want to become". It is aspirational. It is what we are sensing in the subtle fields when we connect to the emerging state and the causal plane. It is who we already are in those states, and therefore who we are already becoming. It is about making the implicit explicit. Not surprisingly, it is important to hold circle space strongly in this process. In order to tap into our collective consciousness, we have to be in a place beyond our individual separateness, we have to be connected in deep relationship. This does not have to be a profoundly mystical experience. It really just means "cutting the crap" and getting down to who we really are. It is the job of the Host (the manifestation of the evolutionary leader in this context) to create the conditions for this to happen. Sometimes it requires more of a yang swordsmanship to defend the space; sometimes it requires more of a yin nurturing to invite people into it. Usually it requires a mix of both.

The collective container should transcend and include the people who compose it, so it is useful to start with the people who are there. Before starting to explore the collective purpose, we often have individuals tune in to their own purpose in this context. Who do they most want to become here? After expressing these individual purposes around the circle, we can explore what is at the centre. What is it that connects and surpasses all those individual purposes? What core purpose lies at the centre of this group?

The simplest way to facilitate this, holding the circle focus, is to ask for phrases or words from people, and to brainstorm (or soul-storm) them onto a flipchart. It is sometimes useful to remind people that they are speaking as and for the whole here, not from their own agendas. Call in the centre whenever you feel that the focus is being lost. Use chimes if necessary. Sometimes the flow of words dries up by itself, at other times you need to stop it. It actually doesn't matter if you stop it – the essence is in any case beyond what is on the flipchart. But it is always worth asking if there is anyone with a burning point to add before moving on.

The next step is to ask people to look for the patterns that connect all the words on the flipchart. What lies beneath and between all that we have said? Encourage someone to try formulating a phrase or sentence that could be the start of "a clear unambiguous statement of that which we jointly want to become". Again, a reminder about speaking as the whole is often useful at this point. It is important to hold circle space consciously at this point, as the purpose takes shape. It is easy for people to slip into a debate about words and semantics, missing the essence behind it. The monkey-mind breaks the soul connection. Remember to "listen with attention".

At some point, you will have a statement which seems to meet the need. It may be very clear, with everyone suddenly in agreement with what emerges. Or there may still be some doubt. Either way, remind people that the purpose is a "work in progress" which will continue to be developed and refined as we go through the rest of the process, and which must be continually revisited in order to keep it alive and for it to have meaning for the group. This helps people to let go of some of the reservations they may have.

Another way to move on is what we call "vote and note". Once you have a statement of purpose, you ask people to decide whether they are entirely happy with it, whether they have some doubts or questions, or whether they think it fundamentally compromises their integrity. If they are fine with it, they give it a thumbs up, if they have a comment the thumb goes horizontal, and if they have a fundamental objection they give it a thumbs down. Ask for people's vote. Then ask to hear the thumbs-down first, followed by the horizontal thumbs. The thumbs-up we don't need to hear. Thumbs-down or horizontal are often a result of a misunderstanding or a need for more clarity, and once that has been given the objections may resolve themselves.

If there is a fundamental objection, however, you have a number of options. You can try and resolve it there and then (this may be necessary for a thumbs-down). Or you can refer it to a group of "guardians" who volunteer to look after the purpose and principles, keeping them alive for the group. This group can then meet with anyone who would like to later on. From experience, leaving things to rest for a while can actually help many people to resolve their resistance, which may have nothing to do with the purpose itself, but more to do with something that has happened between individual participants during the process.

Either way, it is essential to be aware of the integrity of the purpose that has emerged from the Presencing space. That integrity should not be compromised in an attempt to include everybody. It may be that someone's thumbs-down cannot be adequately resolved, and that a way must be found for that person to either release their reservation or gracefully leave the group. Articulating a purpose is part of creating the container. A container has boundaries. Boundaries create the space in which we can work. The nature of boundaries is that some people fall inside and some outside. Boundaries must be held with both integrity and openness. They must never become vague or unclear. We must be conscious about expanding or restricting our boundaries. If some people find themselves falling outside particular boundaries, then it is better for both the group and the individual that they find another context and a better fit elsewhere.

Principles

Once a collective purpose has been established, the next step is to develop a set of principles which support us on our way towards the purpose. Dee Hock defines principles as "a behavioural aspiration of the community, a clear, unambiguous statement of a fundamental belief about how the whole and the parts intend to conduct themselves in pursuit of the purpose". Principles, then, are signposts to guide us on our journey, which we all agree on, and which we can remind ourselves and each other of on the way. Together with the purpose, they create the invisible container (the collective interior lower-left quadrant), out of which the visible structures can manifest. As such, they must come first, before the structures. Structure must emerge out of passion. It doesn't work the other way round.

To facilitate the emergence of principles, we often use a combination of World Café and Appreciative Inquiry. Appreciative Inquiry is an approach to conversation and change that stresses people's best experiences, and looks to draw on those to help shape the future. The first question in the Café is an example of this. We would ask people to share what their best experience has been of living the purpose that they collectively identified. We may include one round of more general sharing of what they heard from each other before moving on to ask them to identify and share what the conditions were that enabled them to have that experience. After another round of asking them to share patterns they have been hearing, we might ask each table to come up with a list of principles inspired by the conversations they have just had about their best experience and the conditions necessary to make it happen.

The key to this process is that the principles arise out of people's *experience*, and are not just nice ambitions plucked from the air. The power of having them come from experience is that we know that we can live them already.

There are various ways of identifying the patterns and connections between the principles that the different tables identify, by clustering them and finding the essence of each cluster. For example, each table could be asked to write each principle on one piece of paper. All the papers are brought back to the circle, where each one is read out and placed in the centre. As they are placed in the centre, people can start to group them, putting them next to others that seem to be similar. They could of course all end up in one group, so encourage people to look for connections but also to keep useful distinctions. Check that people are happy with the groupings, and make any adjustments that need to be made whilst maintaining the integrity of each cluster and of the original individual principles. Then ask people to stand by the cluster that they feel most drawn to, that they feel is most important. Have them go away in those groups, taking all the papers from their cluster with them, and come up with one statement of principle that captures the essence of that group. Bring the synthesised principles back to the group, read them out and list them up, check for clarifications (not disagreements), and then vote and note as for the purpose. Having created and articulated the principles, the purpose should be revisited to see if it has changed in the meantime. There are of course many other ways to elicit principles, but hopefully this gives you a flavour of a process that has worked for us.

This process of clarifying purpose and principles can be done in a day, or it may need periodic sessions over a few months. We have experienced both, depending on the conditions – in particular on how new this way of working is for people. It is important to remember that the purpose and principles should continually evolve, being revisited at every meeting, and re-worked at regular intervals or whenever the group feels the need. It is useful to identify some "guardians" who will be specifically responsible for this.

People

In exploring needs and defining purpose and principles, we are creating the invisible container for the new system. This is the interior glue that connects people together. As such, it has a certain resonance. The quest now is to find the other people who resonate with it. This includes people who work inside the organisation, as well as those with whom the organisation will be interacting – its partners and target group. The questions to clarify at this point are "who are we?" and "who do we need to engage next?"

There are various ways of getting more insight into who we are. We can use models such as Spiral Dynamics to explore the *stage of development* that seems to be active within us. We can also explore what *types* of people we are (types exist at all levels), through models such as the Enneagram and Myers-Briggs typologies. And we can explore the kinds of roles we take in group processes, through for example The Rose of Leary (roles in teams) and the Brain Map (based on Belbin's team roles). The purpose of such explorations is to become clearer on the make-up of the community so far, to be conscious of what we have, where our gaps are and what we may be excluding. This can provide useful insight into who else we may need to invite into the community in order to achieve greater balance.

If the process is unfolding in a change community within an organisation, it is useful at this point to reflect on who else we could engage on the journey. Who are others who already resonate or who might well resonate with what we are doing? We can then start to explore how to engage them, which is where the next steps of Concept and Structure come in. We gradually expand the container of the change community until it becomes the new way of doing things. Each time we engage more people, they need to experience the chaordic design flow to feel its power for themselves. So in an organisation, you might look for a department that you feel is ready to take it on. They will then do a needs check, create their collective purpose and principles, and become conscious of the people, concept and structure that will support those. The idea is that increasing numbers of people will start to organise themselves this way, until it emerges as the conventional way of doing things.

Whenever I think of this process, an image always comes to my mind of a garden pond. Green algae begin to grow on the pond's surface. They continue to multiply. First one, then two, four, eight, sixteen and so on. It looks fairly harmless and we may put off acting on it. But what we forget is that there is only one step between the pond being half covered by algae and it being completely covered. This seems to be how emergence works. Critical mass builds up slowly until suddenly it reaches a tipping point, and then the whole system shifts. So it is that we nurture communities working in a new way within the old system, until the new way suddenly becomes the accepted way of working.

Once the new way has emerged as the new pattern inside the organisation, the next group of people we engage with will be those outside our organisation: our target group or client. Ichak Adizes has an equation for organisational success based on fitness. Success is a function of the relationship between internal integration and external integration. First of all, energy needs to be channelled into internal integration, and only once this is achieved will there be energy to spare for external integration, engaging the outside world. Once the internal organisation is integrated, aligned behind collective purpose and principles, then the energy can shift to the outside.

We can see this in the stages of the S-curve and in Adizes' life cycle. The internal integration starts with Survival and Belonging (Adizes' Courtship and Infant) while the old system is still dominant, then starts to interface with the outside as it completes its integration with the creation of Clear Identity and Bigger Context (Adizes' Go-Go and Adolescence), then finally being fully available to the outside world and creating external integration and fitness with Manifesting New Possibilities and New Insight (Adizes' Prime and Stable).

In the process of internal integration and fitness, each subpart of the organisation creates its own coherence within the bigger whole. Its interior values and exterior structure will depend on what kind of function it must perform. These differences are likely to reflect the patterns of the Spiral Dynamics systems, as described in the section on designing fitness above.

Put simply, interior fitness allows for exterior fitness. It makes total sense if we think about ourselves as well. We are only really available to do our work in the world if we are fit and healthy in ourselves. If we lack fitness, we end up sick at home in bed, and unavailable for the world.

This perspective enables us to help people align themselves with the function and context that best supports them and their current needs behind the bigger purpose of the organisation as a whole. The challenge for the organisation is to define a core purpose that creates enough space for the purposes of the various parts of the organisation and a clear interface with the surrounding world.

In the Imaginal Cells scenario, this stage applies to the change community cell itself. Creating interior fitness is essential before the Cell starts to make itself more visible and engage the organisation more widely. In the Conscious Design Scenario, it applies to the level of organisation that one is working with.

Concept

This phase is about sensing more concretely what an organisational system might look like that would serve the purpose, principles and people identified thus far. This is the crystallising phase in Scharmer's U-process. We are getting a feel for the new organisation.

There are many ways to do articulate a concept. The key is to access people's imagination and creativity. We are not looking for an organisational flowchart, but something that will give us a taste of how it might feel to be part of this organisation. What do we see in our mind's eye? The method you choose will depend on the people you are working with. Methods that we have used at this point include visualisation, drawing, freefall stream-of-consciousness writing, imaginative storytelling and interactive theatre. It raises a lot of positive energy, which carries into the next phase. Keep it light and help people resist the temptation to slip into detailed structural planning. Their time will come next!

Structure

At last we can start to engage with what our organisation it is actually going to look like. In this phase, it is essential to keep the needs, purpose, principles, people and concept present while designing the structure. The structure is there to serve these, and so must flow from them.

In essence, the structures should facilitate an evolving community of practice – which is the next step in the process. The Imaginal Cell becomes a Community of Practice, experimenting and refining the practice of living the future now.

Facilitating Communities of Practice

From the perspective of evolutionary leadership, the aim of any intervention in an organisation is to create a living system which organises itself in response to the needs it senses in its world. In other words, it should spontaneously be doing everything we have talked about in this chapter. Leadership, then, is about holding the space in which this can happen, facilitating the dynamic spiral dance between order and chaos. In order to provide some context around Communities of Practice, we will start by looking at the collective intelligence that such communities both facilitate and grow out of. This means returning briefly to Wilber's lower left "We" quadrant.

The Emergence of Collective Intelligence*

*Having learned ways to quiet their minds and strengthen their health and vitality, aspiring Evolutionary Leaders are ready to dance with the energies of the "We": their teams, communities, and the network of all of their relationships. They are ready to ask and see into powerful questions. For instance:

How can a group of individual intelligences become truly collective intelligence? How can we move forward into a more complex and capable collective intelligence without sacrificing our autonomy?

The act of "seeing into" a powerful question is like holding a baby in your arms and feeling a mix of awe, wonder, and curiosity. Can you hold the following question in that way?

"How can I accelerate the emergence of a higher collective intelligence in a community or organisation that I care for?"

I offer the following definition as a starting point: Collective intelligence is the capacity of human communities to evolve towards higher order complexity and harmony, through such innovation mechanisms as differentiation and integration, competition and collaboration**.

---

* The next two sections are by George Pór.

** Blog of collective intelligence – http://www.community-intelligence.com/blogs/public

Collective intelligence resides in the lower left of Ken Wilber's four quadrants, which is the space of "we," culture and inter-subjectivity. Wilber has sketched out many good maps of that space. Here is an excellent, one-sentence summary: "These shared values, perceptions, meanings, semantic habits, cultural practices, ethics, and so on, I simply refer to as culture, or the intersubjective patterns in consciousness." Steve McIntosh, a student of Wilber's work, has further specified the content of these structures that we share with others in groups:

> *"While the content of subjective consciousness consists of feelings, thoughts, and decisions, the content of intersubjective cultural structures consists of the substance of what is shared by subjective consciousness – the substance of information, meaning, and value."*

In communities and organisations, besides these shared qualities, we also share a capacity to evolve and co-evolve with one another and with the surrounding social, technical, environmental and market ecosystems.

Collective intelligence is continually emerging from the connected conversations in and across social holons*. It is occurring all the time in many invisible ways. Let's make one visible, by way of a simple, small-scale experiment: an open source, collaborative learning process that could give you a taste of collective intelligene in three steps:

---

* Social holons emerge when individual holons commune; they als have a defining pattern (agency or regime), but they do not have a subjective consciousness; instead, they have distributed or intersubjective consciousness. Examples include galaxies, planets, crystals, ecosystems, families, tribes, communities… (ken Wilber)

- Discovering the seed conditions for the emergence of collective intelligence

- Sensing what hinders its evolution

- Comparing notes with other participants

STEP 1. Discovering the seed conditions for the emergence of collective intelligence

We start by asking a focusing question, the answer to which could increase our ability to grow a more robust collective intelligence. For example: what conditions must be present in order for collective intelligence to emerge in communities?

We do not have to build a definitive list of those conditions; we can get to the essentials through a collaborative inquiry, a sort of focused learning conversation. To start this conversation, I suggest considering the following factors.

To amplify its collective IQ, the community needs make its systems and processes available to the benefits of today's Web 2 and Web 3 tools for collaborative knowledge gardening and sensemaking. Those tools enable us to process, portray, and communicate large chunks of information and make meaning out of their constant, kaleidoscopic swirling.

For collective intelligence to emerge, there must also be:

- a shared learning agenda determined by the specific challenges and opportunities that the community wants to address in the short and longer term.

- relationships of trust among members, which liberate the flows of knowledge and value creation.

- frequent opportunities to participate in productive conversations through multiple channels of communication.

What else? What other conditions are also essential to raise our collective IQ?

Do you remember an episode in the life of any of the communities to which you belong or have belonged when you clearly felt the powerful presence of its collective intelligence? What made that moment possible? How did it feel?

STEP 2. Sensing what hinders the evolution of collective intelligence

Evolutionary leaders need to intimately understand not only what fosters collective intelligence, but also the factors that limit its growth.

Collective intelligence doesn't simply evolve. It co-arises with the evolution of four domains: the community's social architecture, its knowledge and learning ecosystem, its economic engine and its technologies for collaboration and coordination. Each of these four domains brings its own set of enablers and obstacles to collective intelligence.

My observation suggests that the potential of communities to evolve toward higher-order integration and capabilities through collaboration and innovation is very limited if:

- ego and turf-battles waste the members' attention and energy,

- conversations are not connected and facilitated for emergence,

- the community's knowledge ecosystem is weak or poorly integrated, so that the cross-fertilisation of ideas, information, and inspirations is sporadic and slow,

- the power of new technologies is not leveraged to compensate for the constraints imposed by cultural, geographical, hierarchical, and other barriers.

In your experience, what are some of the other obstacles to amplifying collective intelligence in organisations?

STEP 3. Comparing notes

I have *collected* my ideas about this thought experiment, and then *connected* them in the 3-phase flow presented here, despite knowing that they are incomplete and sometimes even half-baked. That's just to say, don't hesitate to share yours as they come up rather than waiting for the perfect time to write a polished piece, which may never come. One of the places where you can do that is the Blog of Collective Intelligence*.

A blog is an excellent tool for raising collective intelligence, through the sustained attention that people may give to one another's reflections, intentions and talents.

At the website of the Blog of Collective Intelligence, you can become a blog author by:

---

* http://www.community-intelligence.com/blogs/public/2004/04/the_emergence_of_ci_an_online.html

- posting your insights and questions in the Comments field,

- asking for author rights, which gives you more visibility and connectivity with other bloggers.

Comparing your mental models with others can open the possibility for both individual and collective learning. It is also an accelerator of collective intelligence.

Discovering the common patterns that connect your individually-perceived thoughts is an "Aha!" moment, a moment of collective intelligence discovering itself. Such patterns can be documented in a reflective synthesis provided by "living reports."*

Communities of Practice

To boost collective intelligence to the level required to meet the challenges of our times, we must team up and form learning communities, partnerships, and networks, and we must do so soon if we are to outpace the trends toward fragmentation, devolution and breakdown.

We learn faster and more deeply when we can share our questions and quests with others – not to mention that it is also more fun than the solitary mindset that makes us think we should figure it all out by ourselves.

Evolutionary leaders are expert learners, continually looking for ways to accelerate their learning and the further development of

---

* http://www.community-intelligence.com/node/161.html

their consciousness, compassion, and competence to absorb complexity.

The newest of these ways – communities of practice – is also one of the oldest. Communities of people who learn together from engaging in collaborative inquiries into issues of their shared practice are as old as humanity itself. Only now we are becoming conscious of the need to cultivate them intentionally.

Developing new individual and collective capabilities together, we may also develop friendships that in turn provide the emotional energy of generous attention to one another. When that attention is there, the joy of shared discovery and understanding flows freely among friends and throughout the community.

Communities of practice are self-organising and self-governing groups of people who share a passion for the common domain of what they do and who strive to become better practitioners. Community-based approaches to organising work and developing our capabilities are gaining momentum in many organisations.

> *"Many successful companies are finding that relinquishing some control – specifically by creating the conditions that enable employees to self-organise in virtual communities – is an effective strategy for responding to market pressures. These informal communities – commonly referred to as 'communities of practice' or 'communities of interest' – are steadily proliferating in the workplace today. Organisations that create an environment that supports their formation are gaining significant benefits in the areas of knowledge transfer, response times, and innovation..."**

---

* Collaborative Knowledge Networks: Driving Workforce Performance

Leadership Communities of Practice

There are many kinds of communities of practice, and they come into being in many different ways. In organisations, they frequently develop along the lines of management disciplines, such as R&D, sales, project management, and mentoring.

There are also communities where leaders learn to achieve and sustain their highest potential, supported by one another. Like other communities, leadership communities of practice organise themselves around the shared learning agenda of their members. It may cover one or more leadership territories such as coach/mentor, decision-maker, strategist, communicator, networker, visionary, administrator, and so on.

No matter which territory is the focus of the community's learning agenda, a positive side effect of participating in leadership communities is that members improve their collaborative learning skills, thus becoming more fit to promote a collaborative culture by example.

Evolutionary Leadership Communities of Practice

If we as a species are to meet the challenge of galloping "complexity multiplied by urgency" (Douglas Engelbart), we need to find ways of rapidly developing large numbers of leaders in busi-

---

Through Web-enabled Communities" by Deloitte Consulting, http://www.dc.com/Insights/research/cross_ind/ckn_workforce.asp

ness and society who have the courage and competence to engage with that challenge.

We know from experience that the development of new capabilities is most effective, effortless, and enjoyable when it happens in communities of peers – in networks of mutually supportive relationships among colleagues.

Leaders who step up to the challenge of this gateway decade of our young century need one another's company. Only together can they increase their responsiveness to the need for a shift to a new level of personal, organisational and social evolution. Evolutionary leadership simply means exercising our response-ability to the need to create conditions – in every human institution – that support life's basic patterns of evolution: self-organisation and emergence.

The key to that in organisations is creating conditions for community-enabled strategic results to occur, by liberating the innovation potential of their communities of practice.

Evolutionary leaders tend to form learning communities centred around various areas of their practice, including re-inventing organisational design or cultivating their personal knowledge ecosystem. The boundaries of membership in such communities can span business units, organisations, or industries.

These communities will differ and be defined by their chosen domain of practice. What they will have in common is that they all contribute to evolutionary transformation of whole systems.

The wider the range of fields in which evolutionary leadership is practiced by members of the community, the more potent will be their combined pool of evolutionary competences.

A domain of practice which has a particularly strong influence on an organisation's evolutionary fitness is the "natural design" referred to earlier in this book, the art of applying everything that is applicable from the lessons distilled out of millions of years of biological evolution to facilitating the evolution of our social systems.

How rapidly can the champions of the shift into a new, conscious phase of human and societal evolution develop the new capabilities required to facilitate that transformation? Our future history depends on the answer.

Story

I was invited to help out an 18-strong management team in a major airline. The team was not really a team, but a group of individuals protecting their own turf and negotiating with each other to keep their piece safe. They wanted (and needed!) to become a team. We went through a number of sessions as outlined in the previous chapter. At the end of the final session (prototyping in the U Process), I wasn't sure whether they were going to change or not. In that session I gave them an experience of what it meant to reflect together on their own practice of their principles, and to co-evolve their new behaviour. Then I said that it was up to them now, and that I could do no more for them. They could contact me if they hit any hurdles they wanted help with.

We contacted them a few months later to see how they were doing. Not having heard anything in the meantime, I thought that any learning had probably just dropped away, and that their good intentions had got swallowed up by their everyday busy-ness. However, to our pleasant surprise, they had not only kept up a practice of meeting monthly to reflect on their collaboration as a team in the context of their principles, they were also taking time in their regular meetings to evaluate their process, and had adopted a talking-piece symbolic of the location where we had held most of our sessions. Interestingly, it was not the formal leaders who were making this happen, but people in the group who had resonated most strongly with the approach, and had the personal commitment to take it forward. They were very positive about the changes it was creating in the functioning of their team, even though they recognised that a lot of work still remained to be done.

Where to start

If you are an evolutionary leader and have not yet joined or formed a community, I hope that what you have read so far makes you wonder where to start. A good place is where you are. Compare it to where you want to be, in terms of developing your evolutionary leadership competences. Then think about who else you know who might be at more or less the same stage on their journey. They will be your natural learning partners.

Another good starting point is the "Itch", that felt dissonance with an old way of doing things, followed by a Needs Check and Chaordic Design as outlined earlier in this chapter.

Whatever gives the primary impetus for community formation, in the early, "potential community" stage, you will need to:

● discover your common ground,

● recognise your real passion as a worthy domain,

● find enough potential members to imagine a community,

- understand what knowledge is valuable to share or develop*.

Right after that, you will need to build the capacity for creating the community's technical support system that will enable its social and knowledge architectures. You will need to resource the community. To do so, you will have to learn to generate, facilitate, and connect a network of productive conversations in physical *and* virtual environments.

The competence of designing convivial, vibrant, and life-affirming virtual environments where people can work and grow together, free from the constraints imposed on those processes by restrictive bureaucracies, is *not a technical skill*. It is too important to leave to geeks alone. It is a core competence of evolutionary leadership communities of practice. Not all leaders will know everything it takes to design communities capable of meeting the complexity challenge. It is a *collective* core competence of a leadership community; to support evolutionary transformation, leadership communities must develop expertise in community design.

> "Communities of practice need to be nourished with many different resources. They require ideas, methods, mentors, processes, information, technology, equipment, and money. Each of these is important, but one great gap is that of knowledge, knowing what techniques and processes are available that work well. For example, they may be leading a community development process, yet know nothing of new means to engage the whole community, or new processes for valuing all of a community's assets. Without this knowledge, they either rein-

---

* *Cultivating Communities of Practice*, by E. Wenger, R. McDermott, William M. Snyder

162

vent the wheel, or latch too quickly onto whatever process they hear about, even inappropriate or substandard ones."

The processes of community and knowledge development can and should be enhanced by all the leverage they can get from the new generation of personal publishing and social software.

However:

"Technology's lifesaving and life-changing gifts only make sense when cradled by a network of human conversation, a robust conversation that forms a parallel human network just as powerful as our computer networks, holding any technology to standards of sense and meaning, ethics and personal freedom."

*Does all this raise more questions than answers about the next steps that you need to take in developing the consciousness, compassion, and competence needed to elicit and stage profound transformation? We hope it does, and that you will visit the interactive website of this book, where you can connect, learn, and collaborate with your peers in other organisations, who may have the same questions.

---

* *Supporting Pioneering Leaders as Communities of Practice: How to Rapidly Develop New Leaders in Great Numbers*, by Margaret J. Wheatley, http://www.berkana.org/resources/pioneeringleader.html

** *Crossing the Unknown Sea - Work as a Pilgrimage of Identity*, by David Whyte

Summary of the Imaginal Cells Scenario

In this section we have explored the whole process of enabling a system and organisation to emerge into a new way of being, starting simply from a small group of concerned people.

We started with the Itch, a place where people become aware of an emerging future for which our current way of organising is inadequate. Next we conduct a needs check to see whether other people in the organisation share the same Itch. If they do, we proceed with creating the container that will hold the space for the emergence of the new system. To do this, we follow the U-process and chaordic design flow, which aims to leave us with an organisation with a strong enough identity to create the degree order which will allow the rest of the system to self-organise in response to the evolving world around us. We explore how we currently see the organisation and sense what it means to be a co-creative part of that system. We tune in to the emerging future in order to create our collective purpose, then ask ourselves what principles would best guide us in working towards that purpose.

Next we explore which people are implicated in the venture, and how we can find the best fit-ness for all involved. After that, it is time to get a sense of the concept of the organisation – what will it feel like to work here, what kind of organisation will it be? We then move into creating the practices and structures that will support the people in evolving communities of practice to serve the purpose in line with the principles. All the while we keep checking back that needs, purpose, principles, people, concept, structure and practice are aligned, and we respond appropriately to the feedback we receive. We have achieved an evolving, open, living system of an organisation! For the good of the whole.

Methods for Meaningful Conversations

At this point it is worth introducing some of the methods we have found to be effective at creating the quality of interactive space necessary for the work described above – where authenticity and creativity can flourish. They are just examples of what has worked for us, and should point you more to *the quality of field* we are seeking to create, rather than the details of the methods themselves. You will find the right tools for you and your context.

Circle

The best way I know to create quality space is through circle. Hosting circle simply involves having people sit in a circle, without tables in between them, a beautiful centrepiece in the middle of the circle, some guiding principles, and a few tools of the trade. If held well, this space can create the conditions for deep and powerful communication.

In order to create space, one needs a certain structure – boundaries hold space. The Circle Principles act as part of that structure. We always name them and address them at the start of any circle*.

- Speak with intention

- Listen with attention

- Be aware of your impact on others

---

* These are inspired by PeerSpirit – www.peerspirit.com

STAGES IN EVOLUTIONARY SYSTEMS

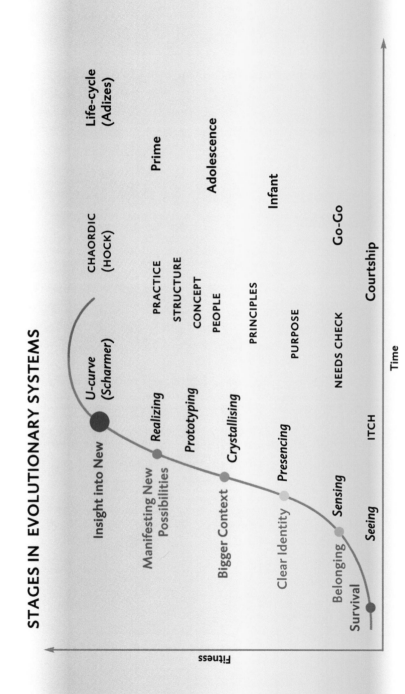

FIGURE 6.12: *Synthesis of Models*

Speaking with intention is about speaking to the centre of the group, speaking as and to the whole, rather than from your own agenda. We know that we are called to speak when we start "quaking" inside (this is where the Quakers got their name from – when we are quaking, the Spirit is moving us). So don't just say anything that pops into your head, but check that the intention is aligned with the centre. If you are well tuned in, the most unexpected things will pop into your head from the centre. Then it's important to voice them. Discernment is the key.

Listening with attention is about listening deeply to what some-one is saying. It means listening beyond the words themselves to the essence of what the person is trying to communicate. We can easily get caught up in words, and start arguing about surface meanings rather than deeper messages. My t'ai chi teacher helped me to see this physically. If in a martial art you focus on the hands of the person who is coming at you, it is hard and stressful to keep yourself centred. However, if you can look beyond their hands to their centre line, shift your focus from their hands to their essence, then it becomes much easier to react to their movements – almost effortless. In this way we are somehow able to witness their movements without being dis-turbed by them, and sense the deeper movements behind. It is the same with words and intention. Just focusing on the words themselves makes it hard for us to get to the deeper meaning behind. Listen deeply to the place people are coming from.

Being aware of our impact on others is about collective respon-sibility for the wellbeing of the group and that which is at its cen-tre. We are looking to co-create something in this space, to con-tribute to the collective flow – like in theatrical improvisation. Look to build on what others have contributed, not to break it down. If what you are going to say is not likely to benefit the whole, then save it until later (or reflect on it later at home).

Setting up these principles with authenticity and lightness can really bring a group into presence, creating the space for deep connection and communication to happen. In a world with so much relativism, it is often a great relief to hear someone

The *centrepiece* also plays an important role. It symbolises that which is at the centre, between all the parts – the spirit of the group that makes it more than the sum of its parts. Directing our attention to the centre of the group rather than to individuals helps to nurture the collective consciousness. In a longer process, it can be powerful to ask people to bring objects to put in the centre, to symbolise the purpose with which they come to the gathering. Candles always add a great quality to the center of the circle.

Some of the *tools of the trade* that can help us to live those principles include a talking piece and a pair of chimes or a bell. A talking piece can be any object, but it is stronger if it is something more symbolic than just a flipchart pen. It is used to create space for people to say what needs to be said without fear of being interrupted. The rule is that whoever holds the talking piece is the only person to talk. Everyone else has the privilege of listening to them. It slows conversations down, giving us time to breathe and digest in between contributions. In normal conversation what often happens is that no sooner has someone started to speak, than what we want to say is already formulating itself in our head. We are no longer able to listen deeply to the other person as we are looking forward too eagerly to hearing our own voice. A talking piece helps to keep us present. As with any tool, it should be used at appropriate moments. The last thing we want is a Tyranny of the Talking Piece!

The bells or chimes also help us to become more present. Tibetan chimes do the job nicely. They cut through noise like a hot knife through butter, and are far more centring than a loud clapping of hands and desperate shout for quiet. We normally use them to open and close Circle. We also announce that anyone who at any time feels that the conversation is becoming decentred, disconnected from the core, can ring the chimes – once to call us into silence, and another time to open the conversation again. People can choose to say why they rang the chimes if they wish to. It is a great way of pausing to take a breath and bringing the focus back to the group. The chimes and talking piece sit in the centre of the circle.

Circle is an approach that can be used at any point in the process, and indeed in any context where people are meeting to have conversations that matter. After a while, it becomes part of the culture of meeting.

The essence of this evolutionary approach to change is that the *solutions to the current problems lie in the people who are themselves part of the system.* They are the parts of the system without which the system would not exist. As such, they carry within them information about the whole. It is not for an external consultant to come in and tell people how they should be, but rather to facilitate the emergence of a future that is already present in the subtle fields.

Intervention processes should therefore aim to do just that – facilitate the emergence of the collective wisdom in the group. An excellent way of doing this is World Café*.

---

* See www.theworldcafe.com

World Café

World Café was developed and named by Juanita Brown and David Isaacs. They identify its principles as:

- Clarify the context

- Create hospitable space

- Explore questions that matter

- Connect diverse perspectives

- Encourage each person's contribution

- Listen together for patterns, insights and deeper questions

- Share collective discoveries

You can see from these principles how World Café contributes to the sensing phase, where we explore the patterns that are present in the collective whole, looking for what lies beneath and between the parts in the subtle fields that can potentially manifest next.

The process is fairly simple. People gather around tables in groups of about three to five, as one might in a café. On each table is a "tablecloth" of paper on which people can draw, write or paint. You can also add a centrepiece and talking piece to each table if it feels appropriate. There are a number of rounds – we normally find that three or four are sufficient. At the end of each round, one person stays behind at the table as the "host", and the others move off to a new table and new people. It is the job of the host to brief the new arrivals on the essence of what happened at that table last round, maybe explaining some of the writings or drawings on the tablecloth. At the end, you gather people back in the whole circle and "harvest" the key insights or learnings from the process.

At the start of each round you ask a question which creates a focus. In the context of a needs check, the first question would be one you had identified with the original group. Each following question aims to build on that and deepen the insight, looking for collective patterns. Steps I have found useful in the past are to ask people to tell each other what they heard others saying (this creates distance from their own opinions and helps to bring their attention to the whole), and then to ask people what patterns they are hearing in the conversations (what seem to be the recurring themes).

As with hosting any process, it is important to be clear with the group about the purpose of the exercise at the outset, and then to come back to it at the end in the harvesting phase. That purpose can frame your question for the final circle. What you do with the outcomes will depend on the context in which are you using the method. It can either be a pure sensing exercise – raising awareness of the whole – or you can use it to come out with concrete recommendations. If you use it for a needs check, it becomes more of a sensing exercise, giving people the space to have the conversations they have been longing to have in their organisation, and getting an idea of what is present in the group. It provides important material for the conversations phase which follows.

Story

Meanwhile, back at the Corporation... it is the first meeting of the change initiative that we call. It's a good turnout. People are present from all the different sections of the unit. Many of them have never spoken to each other. It is a World Café set up, in the organisation's cafetaria. This in itself is a new experience. In the first round, we have them tell each other what they think the need is for this business unit in the world – what is its raison d'etre? We deepen and explore that over three rounds. What emerges is something simple and powerful that they all recognise. That is a strong output in itself, yet the most significant result is the creation of a new experience of the organisation talking to itself. People starting to realise who is in the organisation, what they do, how it all fits together, and what they think this organisation is meant to be doing in the world.

Open Space Technology

Open Space Technology is another way of facilitating conversations in a large group around a collective theme. It was developed and popularised by Harrison Owen. He tells the story of how he used to run large organisational development conferences with speakers and debates, but realised at some point that the most significant conversations happened during the coffee breaks. So he decided to create a meeting process that had all the qualities of a good coffee break!

The structure that creates the open space is itself fairly simple. The quality of that space depends as ever on the interior state of the host (see chapters 3 and 5). Formulating a good question to frame the space is essential. In this phase of needs checking, we are looking for where the need in the world connects to the need of the people in an organisation. The question should engage people's passion and responsibility.

The process works as follows. A schedule is drawn up with time slots and places for people to meet. The subject of each meeting space is left blank, so there is no agenda. People are then asked to host a meeting around a theme that relates to the framing question. Anyone can host a meeting. They may be an expert with something specific to offer, or they may be curious about something they know little about. Their only responsibility as a host is to make sure the workshop happens and to make sure some kind of report comes out of it.

People are invited to write down topics for workshops, announce them to the group and post them somewhere on the matrix of times and locations. This stage continues until either there are no more proposals, or the matrix is full (it can be expanded if there is still great demand). People can then choose which workshops they want to attend.

One law and four principles help to create the structure around the open space. The one law is the Law of Two Feet: if you feel you are neither learning nor contributing, then you should use your two feet to take you somewhere else where you do.

The four principles are:

1 Whichever people come to a workshop are the right people

People are encouraged to take responsibility for what they are passionate about. That is what determines who hosts workshops and who attends workshops. So it is possible that no one goes to a workshop. When this happens, we usually frame it as an opportunity to spend quality time on your own, thinking about something you are passionate about – a luxury we don't often get!

2 Whatever happens is the only thing that could happen.

This invites people to let go of expectations around the outcomes of the workshops, and to be prepared for surprises. Be open to what emerges.

3 Whenever it starts is the right time

Maybe people need to have a chat before they get down to business, or maybe they are fired up to jump right in. Either way, it is a question of not forcing, but of sensing the moment.

4 When it's over, it's over.

If a meeting has served its purpose before the official time is up, then finish up and move on. Likewise, if it is not over at the end of the official time, then arrange another time to continue the conversation.

These are very basic guidelines rooted in common sense, but we seem to find them difficult to practice in our daily lives. If everyone always took responsibility for their passions, then the world would be a much better place! To help people do this, there are two metaphorical creatures that accompany us in Open Space. One is the Bumblebee who buzzes from workshop to workshop, gathering insights here and there and cross-fertilising the wisdom. The other is the Butterfly, who doesn't feel particularly attracted by any of the workshops, and so settles down to sit quietly on their own. They create new spaces, and more often than not another drifting Butterfly will come to rest beside them, and a conversation of great meaning will unfold.

Open Space Technology creates the potential for people to have the conversations that really matter to them. It provides breathing space, and helps a system to hear and see its authentic self more deeply. It connects people to their deeper needs and to the wider world, providing fertile ground for a new life-affirming system to emerge.

The Open Space Rap

Welcome to Open Space,
This is the place
Of a new fashion,
You get to organise
Around your passion!
The task:
To ask
'what really matters to me?'
Then take responsibility
Guided by our core question
Which I am about to mention

READ CORE QUESTION

Let's get this started
'cause this train has already departed
Here's the first mind bender:
We ain't got no agenda!
Yet ...

But I'll bet
in 30 minutes or less
No stress
That wall will be full
And choice will be the tension
In a packed programme guided by our intention:

CORE QUESTION AGAIN

How to do it?
How to fly?
Let me try and
Clarify:
If you got a workshop
to offer to the question
Head to the centre,
Grab a pen and write the intention
Or topic and your name,
To give it some fame
Announce it to us all,
Then take a time and place
And stick it to the wall.
So simple
No trouble at all.
 But here's another mind blaster:
You do not have to be
A master
Expert
Or Mentor.
This here is a curious centre.
If you know nothing
and want to know more,
Don't hold or stop

Host a workshop!
It's a sure
cure
To learn more.

Which brings me to the principles and one law:

'Whoever comes are the right people'
to have around.
They are the ones with the passion
For the ground
You are hoping to cover
Everyone else is searching in the other
Workshops
Serving our core intention.
We working together
In separate places,
It's a great invention!
So, what happens if no-one comes?
All alone.
When was the last time
You got to stop and reflect
On your own?
Especially on something that
Gets you out of your seat
Makes your heart beat.
This time is for your passion
To bring
Unique learning
To us all.
Honour the call.

'Whatever happens is the only thing that could have'
So let go of expectation
Of what this should be,
Set it free.
Trust the open space form
It holds the storm.
 'When it starts is the right is the right time'
It's no crime
To chat or have a cup of tea
Be free and see
When you begin
Don't force it to be happpenin'.

'When it's over it's over'
Don't hang on
Move on
To where you belong.
To fill the time gap
It's a trap
So get up and get movin'
To find a space where
You be contributin'.
You see
this ain't no normal meetin'
Cause we be 'law of two feetin''
 Use your feet
Don't just sit
SPLIT
To move to where you
Learn or share.
So be aware
You can be like the
Humble

Bumble bee,
Tripping from place to place
And cross pollinate,
Connecting info
Helping collective wisdom grow.
One other character
Who arrives with a flutter
Is the butter – fly.
Who hangs out, looking good
As a butterfly should.
A place of still
To stop and reflect
Have the conversation you least expect,
A wonderful insect!

Some final words on
Workshop hosting.
It ain't all coasting!
If you pin it up on the wall
You responsible for that call.
The workshop gotta happen,
Even if you don't go
You responsible for opening the show.

Second thing,
There's only two
(PHEW!)
Please record what is cooking
'cause we all looking
to see
in gallery.
Have no fear it is pretty clear,
There a template set up

for the usin',
Now we're cruisin'
Into the final moments before
Opening the wall
And the market stall.

Just to say again
Grab a paper and pen
Write your workshop
Announce it to us all
Then stick it to the wall
With a time and place,
Take your time
this ain't no race.
With no more ado,
I Open Space ...

Conscious Design Scenario

The difference between this scenario and the Imaginal Cells scenario is that we already have someone in a position of enough responsibility to be able to initiate a change process for an already existing unit, organisation or system. This results in a twin-track approach. The first track is the facilitating emergence approach outlined above, but this time working with everyone involved in the system that the person is responsible for. The second track adds a more hands-on parallel process of assessment and design.

As stated at the start of the chapter, the first thing to do is find out where the system is situated in the change cycle, its potential for change and its place on the Spiral. The second track would be assessing this through individual assessments and interviews, which will then feed into the collective conversations. As the conversations unfold around need, purpose, principles, people, concept and structure, this track would be looking to redesign the systems and structures based on the natural design and fitness principles outlined above.

Given the management capacity in the Conscious Design scenario, we are able to blend the work of collective intelligence and building the new field in the organisational culture, with structural design that aligns functions, people and systems along the Spiral, behind the new purpose and principles.

Ideally there comes a point in the Imaginal Cells scenario where the possibility to add the conscious design element emerges. The two scenarios are really only different in their starting point. Are you starting with a cross-sector of concerned people in the organisation, or are you starting with a person in a position of responsibility for an organisation or entity who sees the need for this kind of change? The answer to that question will determine which approach is most suitable – Imaginal Cells or Conscious Design.

We can also relate the facilitating emergence strategy to the four capacities of the holon, as we explored earlier in the section on designing fitness. A reminder: everything is a holon (a part and a whole) with four major capacities that play out in the individual and collective dimensions:

- "Agency", which is the capacity to clarify identity, wholeness and boundaries, and express that in the world.

- "Communion", which is the capacity to connect to whatever is outside those boundaries.

- "Self-transcendence", which is the capacity to go beyond where one currently is on the evolutionary path.

- "Self-immanence", which is the capacity to hold all one's parts and past together in the present, healing and integrating past patterns.

For designing fitness we needed to focus on the capacities for agency and communion, whereas for facilitating emergence we need to pay attention to the capacities for self-transcendence and self-immanence. Table 6.3 will give you a feel for how you can translate these theoretical concepts into work in our organisations (with thanks again to Diederick Janse for the co-creation).

Once the process shifts into new systems and structures at the top of the U-process, we should have achieved an organisation that meets a real need in the world, that nurtures human spirit and affirms people for who they are, and that contributes to the evolution of the whole. Good for the organisation, good for the people involved, and good for the universe. Evolutionary leadership at work.

Story

Meanwhile, back at the Corporation... it is two years down the line in the work with the business unit, and our change agent is a happy soul. Employee satisfaction has exceeded all historical records, business growth is triple-digit and he has been awarded People Manager of the Year. As I look at the table of interventions above, I see we have literally been working in all those areas. Our integral evolutionary approach is proving itself.

This is important for me, as it is the first major case study we have of application in a business environment. And it is very significant for our Change Agent who has grown immensely in the process. Six months after we started, he took up Zen meditation, and others in the Unit followed suit. It has been a four-quadrant affair, and created a platform for the Unit and our Change Agent to explore a future full of promise. It has also created an example inside a very established Corporation that they are finding hard to ignore.

CHAPTER SEVEN

Stepping into the Flow

Switch it on

Stepping up to voice
My choice
To let it go
The flow
Is beyond control
So when you fall
Roll
Then rise
Open your eyes
See the fresh horizon
Great eastern sun risin'
Resplendent
Transcendent
Heaven sent
An extension
To the new dimension
The fourth perspective
Reflective
Of the so far unseen
Subtle being
The place from which Gandalf and Arthur ride
Where secret valleys hide
Where Isaiah spoke messiah

The second coming is the inner fire
Walkin' the wire
To paradise lost in the frost
It's the time of the great turning
Great burning
Great thaw I am sure
The final unmasking
Now I'm askin':

What if it's been there all along?
And we just never switched it on?

Shangri La is not far
Shambhala, Camelot glory
The Atlantis story
Dante's peak of mount purgatory
The new birth of heaven here on earth
The Ultimate wave to surf
The place of shift
Where we all uplift
Into the fourth dimension

Paradise is not hidden in the ice
It's here
Beyond the fear
The next tier
The fog begins to clear
To reveal
A divine seal
As we fall,
Roll and rise waking up to the higher call
Open our eyes to the stars
Walk through the mirage

Onto solid ground
Paradise found.
What if it's been there all along?
And we just never switched it on?
Paradise found

Heroes abound
Sensing the future with sonar sound
Cutting the path
Being the pavers
Removing the layers
Of deception
Perception
Peeling back reality
To the feelin' inside of me
Of future generations calling us on
The wind in the sails of a ship in a storm
Life momentum
Never endin'
Waves from behind
Echoes in mind
Nagging unease
This itchin' ain't fleas
It's the future coming in on the breeze.

What if it's been there all along?
And we just never switched it on

The field beyond right and wrong
That's where we belong
That's where we been all along
I ain't no car salesman
This ain't no con

It's a revelation
In every nation
On every station
Since creation
Just switch it on

So what do you reckon? Are you up for it?

It is time for one last, quick recapitulation. We have looked at the bigger picture of how everything hangs together as a dynamic, evolving whole. We have got a sense of what it might feel like to live our lives from that place of freedom and wholeness, and how we can get support from our physical organism to do that. We have also explored the exciting prospect of being in that space together with others, the creative collective power that it can unleash. And finally we've looked at some different tools and processes which we can use to organise ourselves in that light. Figure 7.1 shows how it all looks on Wilber's quadrants.

An important part of my purpose in writing this book was to bring together the experience of being in a space of freedom and wholeness with the hard technologies we can use to manifest the work in the world. The evolutionary leadership perspective is not about just a nice sense of bliss and happiness. It implies a commitment to make it real in every part of our lives. Resting in radical emptiness, we also embrace all form. Form is evolving. Evolution is a messy if beautiful business. It doesn't all go in nice linear progression as some of the maps I have used above might suggest if taken too literally. However, there are methods and processes which people have been developing and working with in the real world which facilitate evolution and emergence. They are out there. If we are really serious about committing ourselves to this perspective and way of being, we will have to step away from our meditation cushions and move out to engage our world – which will meet us where we are and help us take the next steps.

Transcending the world of matter into blissful oneness is the easy part. Re-engaging the world of matter from that place is the challenge. It is only when we re-engage, when we truly explore a place of non-duality, that we learn what it is all about. As we enter the world with our firm intentions, we will be challenged every step of the way. Mirrors will be held up to reflect back at us our deepest darkest corners. If we face what we see in ourselves and in the world, we will be truly transformative evolutionary leaders. If we shy away, we will be part of the old problems. It takes courage, humility and commitment. It brings huge liberation and transformation – for us as individuals and for us as the world.

From where I now stand, there is simply nothing else to do. As a participant said on one of our leadership courses, echoing Martin Luther – "Here I stand, I can do no other". Those words still stay with me. "Trust" is the angel card I picked this morning. The angel in the picture feeds the unicorn from her hand. Trust in the universe and the universe will meet us – and we will meet our Original Face.

That is the interior driver for me. That sense has to be present. It keeps me connected, centred and engaged. We then engage with the world as we find it.

The next three sections start to make the case for evolutionary leadership to three main sectors of society: business, civil society and the public sector. They are not meant to be comprehensive, but point to how we present the approach in different ways to respond to the different surface needs of various players in the world. You can do the same for the context most relevant to you.

Engaging Business

The following points emerged from conversations we had with a small group to explore this question:

- Business spends billions of dollars every year on training and development (T&D). The low return on that investment is common knowledge in management. It is so, in part, because of the lack of an evolutionary context; T&D funds are rarely directed to meet an evolutionary tension. Liberating some of those dollars to support the evolutionary impulse is a possibility, therefore a responsibility.

- Companies that demonstrate success in the long term are woven from threads of right relationship to employees, partners, and the marketplace. Business success will most likely be increased when those interpersonal and inter-organisational relationships are based on universal principles of fitness and evolution.

- Mergers and acquisitions, strategic alliances, and value chains are examples of companies moving toward ever-greater complexity and integration. When driven by collective ego needs, their integration does not fulfil its potential. Within the evolutionary context leaders, can intuit the true potential of those integrations to create value.

- Given management's general lack of insight into how to cope with the exponentially accelerating pace of change, there is a growing demand for ways of creating meaningful and productive conversations, such as the Circle method, Communities of Practice, deep learning conversations, and

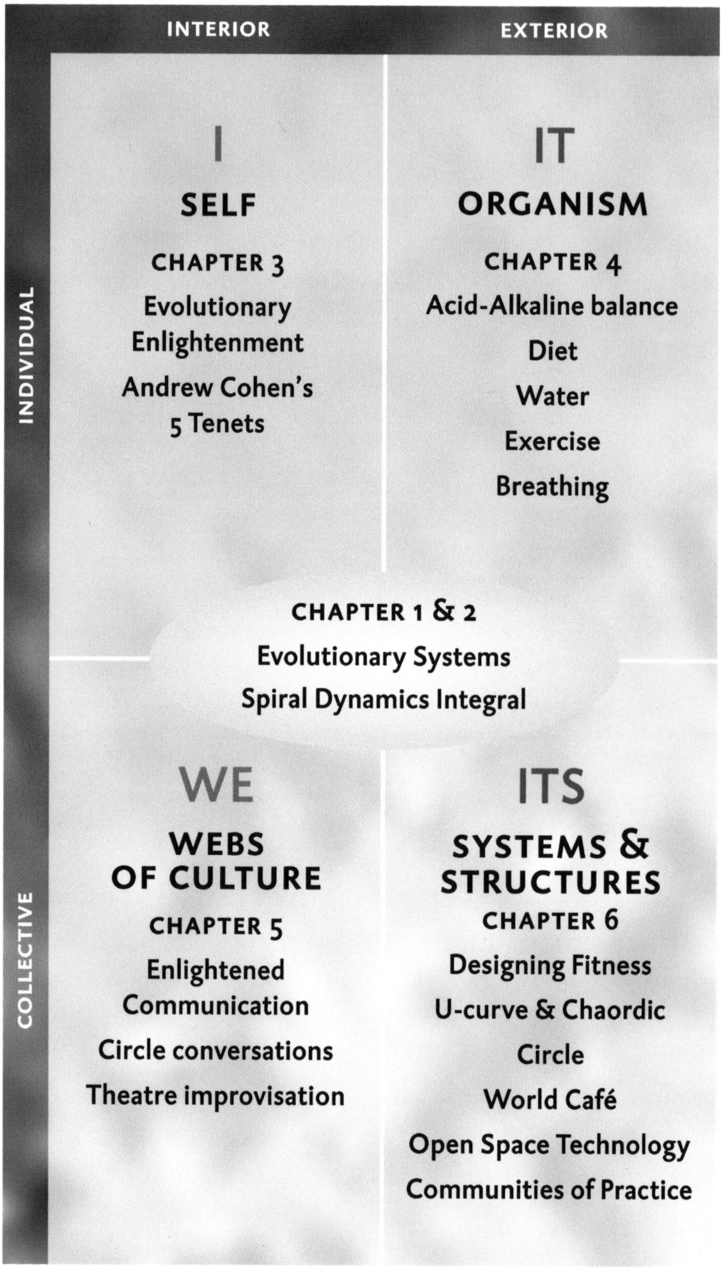

	INTERIOR	EXTERIOR

INDIVIDUAL

I
SELF

CHAPTER 3

Evolutionary
Enlightenment

Andrew Cohen's
5 Tenets

IT
ORGANISM

CHAPTER 4

Acid-Alkaline balance

Diet

Water

Exercise

Breathing

CHAPTER 1 & 2

Evolutionary Systems

Spiral Dynamics Integral

COLLECTIVE

WE
WEBS
OF CULTURE

CHAPTER 5

Enlightened
Communication

Circle conversations

Theatre improvisation

ITS
SYSTEMS &
STRUCTURES

CHAPTER 6

Designing Fitness

U-curve & Chaordic

Circle

World Café

Open Space Technology

Communities of Practice

FIGURE 7.1: *Wilber's Four Quadrants (2000)*

the art of powerful questions. The art of Enlightened Communication would respond to a real need.

- If a significant minority of businesses learns to operate as communities of free agents who live in, and act from, their Authentic Selves, they can become the tip of the evolutionary wave and benefit from "first-mover" advantages in multiple ways. Companies embracing and embodying the principles of evolutionary leadership will create opportunities for themselves, the size and positive business impact of which will greatly surpass today's speculative opportunities framed by the short-term thinking of the company's collective ego.

- Leadership work based on the principles of evolutionary leadership will create surprising results. One that we can expect is the ease with which business leaders will be able to create working environments that will bring the best out of all members of the organisation and free them by a natural process from those who do not want to evolve.

The key point is that people are sensing a need in the world for things to be done differently. The old systems feel inadequate. Speaking to the head of Corporate Social Responsibility (CSR) at a large pharmaceutical company, I asked him why they were investing so much in CSR. His reply was both surprising and heartening. He said that they had realised that the people with the most creative and innovative minds, particularly the younger generation, were not going to work for an organisation that was exploiting people and planet.

Along with second-tier cognitive complexity come second-tier values. The successful businesses of tomorrow will be those which tune in and respond most quickly to this emerging need.

Evolutionary leadership is responding to an emerging need and the sooner businesses do likewise, the more quickly they will be able to capitalise on it as market leaders. The difference with old business practice is that in order to do so they will have to find ways of truly embracing people, planet and profit. Given that people and planet are evolving systems, evolutionary leadership fits the bill.

Engaging Civil Society Organisations

Most of the above points also apply to civil society organisations (csos). Traditionally many campaigning and advocacy organisations get stuck in old "blame and be blamed" dynamics, polarising the world between goodies and baddies (with them as the goodies of course). Getting off our high horses and understanding ourselves as intrinsically connected parts of the same evolving whole enables us to engage with other actors in society as we find them. Everything emerges for a reason, in response to a need – businesses as much as csos. Without losing our vision and commitment for a better world, we can understand the deeper dynamics of evolutionary change and apply pressure in the right places at the right time. It makes us far more effective; we radiate a more dynamic rather than grumpy image, and attract members from more levels of society. So many causes become bandwagons for our egos, helping to maintain a false sense of separation between ourselves and others. We really need to move beyond this if we are to co-create a future worthy of who we truly are.

A couple of verses from a song called *Water, Fire and Smoke* by John Seed come to mind:

I lay down my burden, the weight of my years,
Gods I have worshipped and causes held dear.
For who will I be when they all disappear
Into water, fire and smoke?
I've knelt in the ashes, in peace may I rise,
Empty of knowing and full of surprise,
Clothed all in silence, a baby baptised
Into water, fire and smoke.

When we become too involved in a single cause or issue, there is great risk that we stay static as the world moves on. The cause becomes something that we cling to in order to satisfy our need for identity. We become dependant on it, rather that engaging with it from a place of wholeness. And because we identify ourselves so strongly with it, whenever it gets criticised by anyone, we feel our own identity is under threat, and often respond with an aggression which is far removed from the values of tolerance and respect that we so proudly proclaim.

Evolutionary Leadership in civil society organisations would radically transform the way they engage with the world. There would be congruence between what is preached and practised. Activists would hold great compassion whilst also wielding the knife of insight with great precision. A huge weight is lifted off our shoulders when we no longer have to save the world. In fact, the world will save us. Letting go, we stop struggling and feel the fresh breeze of life on our faces.

Engaging the Public Sector

We have seen that businesses and civil society organisations alike have everything to gain from adopting evolutionary leadership. Public organisations linked to government structures are no different. From my experience, while the issues that such bodies are dealing with are generally different, the implications are the same. Organisations linked to government seem by their nature to be structured in a very ordered, hierarchical way. This is partly the nature of policy implementation. The politicians decide what must happen, and the executive must follow their orders and implement their decisions. Politicians are usually held responsible for something if it goes wrong, and that goes into the public domain, so there is great fear about loss of face. This fear is often passed on to those at the top of the public organisation, whose response is to try to control as much as possible of what goes on. Remembering the four interlinked chaordic circles, this need for control creates apathy in those below because they do not feel like they are being trusted or given responsibility. It makes the organisation slow and cumbersome (the stereotypical traits of a bureaucracy) because everything has to go up to the top before it can be acted on.

Politicians are actually interested in efficiency of implementation, so that the people will actually *feel* the impact of decisions taken in parliament. This being the case, a command-control (Spiral Dynamics Blue) organisation is not the best solution. Creating a chaordic organisation working with evolutionary leadership would enable the organisation to keep and enhance its sense of public service (in its Purpose and Principles), thus ensuring the motivation and response-ability of the employees. With that commitment and identity in place, those at the top could let go of control, enabling those below to self-organise to carry out the work that needs to be done. They would feel that their insight is respected, and that they are trusted to do their best. When people feel trusted like this, they give of their best and produce the best results. There is a shift from an inward-focused, overly structured bureaucracy to an outward-focused, dynamic and self-organising living system, with its sensors in the real world of the citizen and its deep commitment to public service. What more could we want?

In conclusion, these are some ways that businesses, civil society organisations and the public sector could benefit from the evolutionary leadership perspective. There are surely many more, and a strong case to be made for many other contexts. In the bigger picture, introducing evolutionary leadership would mean more organisations increasingly tuned in to what is actually happening in the world, motivated to respond to that reality, and creating a healthier place to live. It would mean people spending a much greater part of their lives in more life-affirming working environments, where our natural connectedness to the world around us is honoured and our unique contribution is supported and manifested. They would inevitably bring this atmosphere home to their families. In short, we would become species and society more in tune with who we really are, and therefore more likely to act in ways which support that. An increased chance of survival. More fit-ness all round.

Apart from all that, it's just great to feel oneself coming back to life.

The Beginning

I wrote this book because this is where I am at. It is my own learning edge. It is the terrain that I am exploring in the world and in myself. As I think back over the book, I remind myself that it is important to take it all lightly. This does not mean abandoning the clarity of intention that is needed. It means recognising that on the one hand we are already always perfect, and on the other hand there is no such thing as perfection here on Earth. Either way, there is absolutely no point in trying to be perfect, because we already are, and because that state of perfection cannot exist in Samsara.

So I invite you to play with the ideas and approaches in this book. Experiment and create your own way of being and doing the work you are called to do. This book is what I have to offer at this time. By the time you read this, I will have moved on. I always love to engage with fellow travellers, so feel free to connect more physically through the Evolutionary Leadership website (www.evolutionary-leadership.com).

Bon voyage. It's time to begin.

Story

Meanwhile, back at the CHE... 3 years since we started, we have settled into a new culture and structure. We are busy applying an integral evolutionary perspective to challenges in the Netherlands and the world. We are learning what it means to integrate first-tier value systems into an organisation from a second-tier perspective. And we continue to live as an experiment, moving forward whilst learning all the time.

I am beginning to understand what it means to be fully engaged and totally free as a leader, and how those two positions reinforce each other. It all feels very exciting and new on the one hand, and the most natural thing in the world, on the other. To use a quote that Margaret Wheatley shared recently, we will simply "proceed until apprehended".

Superman

This is about the cravin'
for savin'
Wanting to control the rampant misbehavin'
Breaking the shackles of all the enslavin'

Break it down
Gather round
Cause we messin' up the earth
Tearing up the turf
The place is our birth
Right
Someone turn on the light
Cause we all fightin'
In the dark
Thinking we be Clark
Kent
Heaven sent
To do it our way
I got news
I just gotta say
There is a master plan
Listen if you can
Take off the stupid costume
You ain't superman.
Hero
No
Let go
Tune into the deeper flow
Into the phonebox
Strip off
Even the socks

Standing naked
Remove the layers
Walls
Safety nets
Take off all the bets
Keep burrowing down
Till you hit original ground
Where all was created from
Before time ran
And history began
Before thinking stirred
Before thought occurred.

It is vast
No dye is cast
No choice is made
No roles played
Beyond the clash
Bang bash
Mish mash
Of evil and good
Shouldn't and should.
The field
Beyond right and wrong
That's where I belong
That's where I been all along.

From here
It is clear
No fear
Just a lashin'
of compassion.
The invisible structure to life on top

What soil is to the crop
What field is to the yield
It is tragic
We forget this magic.

Out of the box
Not even wearing socks
Naked to the core
Wounds raw
Soul sore
Ready to explore
The new Shore

(TIM MERRY)

Bibliography and Resources

Adizes, Ichak (1999), *Managing Corporate Lifecycles*, Prentice Hall Press, New Jersey.

Barrett, Richard (1998), *Liberating the Corporate Soul*, Butterworth Heinemann, Philadelphia.

Beck, Don (2001), *The Global Great Divide*, Institute for Values and Culture, Texas.

Beck and Cowan (1996), *Spiral Dynamics*, Blackwell, Oxford.

Bloom, Howard (2000), *Global Brain*, John Wiley & Sons, Toronto.

Cohen, Andrew (2000), *Embracing Heaven and Earth*, Moksha Press, Lenox USA.

Cohen, Andrew (2002), *Living Enlightenment*, Moksha Press, Lenox USA.

Colbin, Annemarie, (1986), *Food and Healing*, Ballantine Books, New York.

Emoto, Masaru (2003), *Messages from Water*, HADO, Kyoikusha.

Graves, Clare (2002), *Levels of Human Existence*, ECLET

Publishing, Santa Barbara.

Hock, Dee (1999), *Birth of the Chaordic Age*, Berrett-Koehler, San Francisco.

Kurzweil, Raymond (2001), *The Law of Accelerating Returns* *http://www.kurzweilai.net/articles/art0134.html?printable=1*

Laszlo, Ervin (2001), *Macroshift: Navigating the Transformation to a Sustainable World*, McGraw-Hill Education, Hightstown.

Macy, Joanna; Molly Young Brown (1999) *Coming Back to Life*, New Society Publishers, Gabriola Island.

McTaggart, Lynne (2001), *The Field*, HarperCollins, London.

Millman, Dan (2000) *The Way of the Peaceful Warrior*, HJ Kramer, California.

Murphy, Michael (1994) *The Future of the Body*, JP Tarcher, Los Angeles.

Owen, Harrison (1997) *Open Space Technology: A User's Guide*, Berrett-Koehler, San Francisco.

Scharmer, O, *Theory U* (forthcoming) – see also www.ottoscharmer.com.

Senge, Scharmer, Jaworski, Flowers (2004), *Presence: Human Purpose and the Field of the Future*, Society for Organizational Learning, Cambridge USA.

Sheldrake, Rupert (2000), *The Presence of the Past: Morphic*

Resonance and the Habits of Nature, Inner Traditions International, Rochester USA.

Stewart, John (2000), *Evolution's Arrow : The Direction of Evolution and the Future of Humanity*, The Chapman Press, Canberra.

Rischard, J-F (2002), *High Noon – 20 Global Problems, 20 Years to Solve Them*, Basic Books, New York.

Wheatley, Margaret (1999), *Leadership and the New Science*, Berrett-Koehler, San Francisco.

Wilber, K (2000). *A Theory of Everything*, Gateway, Dublin.

Wilber, K (2000). *Integral Psychology*, Shambhala Publications, Boston.

Wilber, K (1981). *Up from Eden*, Theosophical Publishing House, Wheaton.

People Referenced

Here are some more details of people I have come across on my journey (either in face-to-face or through their work) who have influenced my thinking, and whom I have referred to in the book.

Dr Ichak Adizes

Dr. Adizes is one of the world's leading experts on improving the performance of business and government by making fundamental changes without the chaos and destructive conflict that plague many efforts. Over the past 35 years, he has worked with some of the largest commercial organizations in the world and consulted with many heads of state. Dr. Adizes is the Founder and CEO of the Adizes Institute, a highly specialized, change management organization with offices in the United States and 14 other countries around the world. He is also a noted author and has lectured in four languages in over 40 countries.

Adizes' work has been featured in *Inc. Magazine, Fortune,* the *New York Times, London Financial Times, Investor Relations Daily, Nation's Business and World Digest.* He is the author of seven books that have been translated into 22 languages. His *Corporate Lifecycles: How Organizations Grow and Die and What to Do About It (1988)* is regarded as a classic in management theory and was selected as one of the 10 Best Business Books by The Library Journal. A revised edition was published under the title *Managing Corporate Lifecycles* in 1999. Dr. Adizes' other books include the *Pursuit of Prime (1996)*, *Mastering Change: The Power of Mutual Trust and Respect in Personal Life, Family, Business and Society (1992)*, *How to Solve the Mismanagement Crisis (1979)*, and *Self-Management (1975)*. Dr. Adizes has a Ph.D. and M.B.A. from Columbia University and a B.A. from Hebrew University. (from www.adizes.com)

Dr Don Beck

Dr Don Beck is a Co-founder of The National Values Center, Denton, Texas; CEO of The Spiral Dynamics Group; and Founder of the Institute for Values and Culture. He is also a Member of: the American Psychological Association, the World Future Society, the International Paleopsychology Project, and the "Cadre-of-Experts on Ethnopolitical Violence," named by the American and Canadian Psychological Associations. Fellow of the George Gallup Institute at Princeton. He was adjunct Professor at the Conoco Corporate University for two years and is presently on the faculty of the Adizes Graduate School in Santa Barbara, California.

Beck is the co-author of *The Crucible: Forging South Africa's Future* (with Graham Linscott, l991) and *Spiral Dynamics: Mastering Values, Leadership & Change* (with Christopher Cowan, l996). He also wrote a "Sports Values" column for the *Dallas Morning News* for six years. He appears often in the US media regarding issues related to values, sports, and racial divides.

Beck was named Outstanding Professor at the University of North Texas in l978; named an Honor Professor in l979; and listed as an "Outstanding Educator in America" in l980. Beck taught for 20 years at the University before resigning his professorship to work behind-the-scenes in the South African transformation. He made 62 trips to Johannesburg between l981 and

2002, and had a significant impact on political leaders, the business sector, religious leadership, and the general public. He was honoured in 1996 by a joint resolution of the Texas House and Senate with the words: "The Texas House and Senate takes great pride in commending a truly remarkable Texan, Dr. Don Edward Beck, for his invaluable contributions toward the peaceful creation of a democratic South Africa."

Don is also a great friend and a man with a huge heart.
drbeck@attglobal.net ; www.spiraldynamics.net

Dieuwke Begemann

Dieuwke Begemann's work is about letting go of what is holding one back and starting anew. She works with change processes. Two aspects of change have influenced her the most, and form the basis of her philosophy.

Firstly an insight that she gained from eastern martial arts. Someone who is focused on what they want and sees it in a positive light will have a lot more strength in the fight that someone who is focused on resisting. That is why she helps people and organisations to find their strength by working on a positive picture of the future.

From her experience, she also has a deep trust in spontaneous change processes. Change happens by itself, from the inside out. She draws inspiration from her sense of connection to the natural world, which is growing all the time – as we are. She feels our belonging to nature not just in our bodies but also in our spirit and soul. She works with "organic change" – looking to unblock the natural flow of creative energy.

begemann@antenna.nl – www.begemannconsultancy.nl

Howard Bloom

Howard Bloom, a Visiting Scholar at New York University, is founder of the International Paleopsychology Project, executive editor of the New Paradigm book series, a founding board member of the Epic of Evolution Society, and a member of the New York Academy of Sciences, the National Association for the Advancement of Science, the American Psychological Society, the Human Behavior and Evolution Society, The International Society of Human Ethology, and the Academy of Political Science. He has been featured in every edition of *Who's Who in Science and Engineering* since the publication's inception.

In 1981, Bloom organized the material he'd unearthed [in his work so far] and began the formal research for a new theoretical structure that would first reveal itself in *The Lucifer Principle: A Scientific Expedition Into the Forces of History.* However he continued pursuing scientific truths in unconventional ways. In 1995 Bloom headed an insurgent academic circle called "The Group Selection Squad" whose efforts precipitated radical re-evaluations of neo-Darwinist dogma within the scientific community. In 1997, he founded a new discipline, paleopsychology, whose participants included physicists, psychologists, microbiologists, paleontologists, entomologists, neuroscientists, paleoneurologists, invertebrate zoologists, and systems theorists. Paleopsychology's mandate is to "map out the evolution of complexity, sociality, perception, and mentation from the first 10(-32) second of the Big Bang to the present."

Evolutionary biologist David Sloan Wilson has written that with his unusual insights Bloom has "raced ahead of the timid scientific herd" often "vaulting over their heads" with a "grand vision" that "we do strive as individuals, but we are also part of something larger than ourselves, with a complex physiology and mental life that we carry out but only dimly understand." In *The*

Lucifer Principle and his new book *Global Brain: The Evolution of Mass Mind from the Big Bang to the 21st Century*, Howard Bloom brings those understandings from dimness into the light.

(from www.howardbloom.net)

Andrew Cohen

Andrew Cohen has been a teacher of enlightenment since 1986. He is the author of twelve books on the spiritual life, and founder of the award-winning magazine *What is Enlightenment?* In his eighteen-year odyssey as a teacher, Cohen has forged an independent path in pursuit of truth. His own teaching has been lauded as one of the most original and complete contemporary expressions of awakened understanding. And perhaps most notably, he has captured the imagination of the modern spiritual world by igniting a dynamic international dialogue in the pages of his groundbreaking magazine *What Is Enlightenment?* Ceaselessly questioning his own experience and observing the examples of others, Cohen has emerged as a defining voice in the quest to understand what it means to seek – and attain – enlightenment in the twenty-first century. He continually travels the world giving talks and extended retreats and meeting with spiritual leaders and visionaries from every tradition.

(from www.andrewcohen.org)

Kees Hoogendijk

Kees Hoogendijk received his masters degree in chemical engineering from the Technical University in Delft the Netherlands in 1970.He held several positions in the oil and chemical industry, prior to starting his own chemicals trading business in 1982. In 1992 he sold his business to Enron and worked with Enron in several senior posts in the Houston office. After an intense learning period of two years, he left Enron in 1994 to start his own venture capital firm Kegado (*Kees gaat duurzaam ondernemen* (Kees goes into sustainable business)). Kegado invests in starting sustainable business initiatives. Kees believes that sustainability is best served by business solutions that address the ever-increasing social, cultural and environmental frictions at the same time espousing sound financial principles. Current initiatives in Kegado include a customer care centre employing women re-entering the labour market, a company called Business for Climate that markets green climate-neutral products to enhance public awareness regarding global warming, a company called Vital4Life that coaches private individuals and company employees in adopting a healthier lifestyle and a company called Ohm ElectroCare, that offers measurements and technical solutions to minimize the potential harmful effects on people from electromagnetic radiation emitted by electronic devices. Kees's interests are focussed in the area where science, business and spirituality meet. He believes that mankind is on the threshold of making major technological breakthroughs in quantum, vacuum and plasma physics that will offer fundamental solutions for many of the worlds current problems.

khoogend@xs4all.nl ; www.vital4life.nl

Ray Kurzweil

Ray Kurzweil was the principal developer of the first omni-font optical character recognition, the first print-to-speech reading machine for the blind, the first CCD flatbed scanner, the first text-to-speech synthesizer, the first music synthesizer capable of recreating the grand piano and other orchestral instruments, and the first commercially marketed large-vocabulary speech recognition. Ray has successfully founded and developed nine businesses in OCR, music synthesis, speech recognition, reading technology, virtual reality, financial investment, cybernetic art, and other areas of artificial intelligence. All these technologies continue today as market leaders. Ray's Web site, KurzweilAI.net, is a leading resource on artificial intelligence.

In 2002 Ray Kurzweil was inducted into the National Inventors Hall of Fame established by the U.S. Patent Office. He received the $500,000 Lemelson-MIT Prize (view the video), the nation's largest award in invention and innovation. He also received the 1999 National Medal of Technology, the nation's highest honor in technology, from President Clinton in a White House ceremony. He has also received scores of other national and international awards, including the 1994 Dickson Prize (Carnegie Mellon University's top science prize), Engineer of the Year from Design News, Inventor of the Year from MIT, and the Grace Murray Hopper Award from the Association for Computing Machinery. He has received twelve honorary Doctorates and honors from three US presidents and seven national and international film awards. His book, The Age of Intelligent Machines, was named Best Computer Science Book of 1990. His best-selling book, The Age of Spiritual Machines, When Computers Exceed Human Intelligence, has been published in nine languages and achieved the #1 best selling book on Amazon.com in the categories of "Science" and "Artificial Intelligence." Ray's upcoming book, coauthored with Terry Grossman, M.D. is "Fantastic Voyage: Live Long Enough to Live Forever," published by Rodale.

(from www.KurzweilAI.net)

Professor Ervin Laszlo

Ervin Laszlo is the author or editor of 69 books translated into as many as 19 languages, and has over 400 articles and research papers and six volumes of piano recordings to his credit. He serves as editor of the monthly *World Futures: The Journal of General Evolution* and of its associated *General Evolution Studies* book series.

Laszlo is generally recognized as the founder of systems philosophy and general evolution theory, serving as founder-director of the General Evolution Research Group and as past president of the International Society for the Systems Sciences. He is the recipient of the highest degree in philosophy and human sciences from the Sorbonne and the coveted Artist Diploma of the Franz Liszt Academy of Budapest. His numerous prizes and awards include four honorary doctorates.

Laszlo serves as president of the Club of Budapest. He is an advisor to the UNESCO Director General, ambassador of the International Delphic Council, member of the International Academy of Science, World Academy of Arts and Science, and the International Academy of Philosophy. He is the former president of the International Society for Systems Sciences.

(See www.club-of-budapest.org)

Joanna Macy

Eco-philosopher Joanna Macy, Ph.D., is a scholar of Buddhism, general systems theory, and deep ecology. She is also a leading voice in movements for peace, justice, and a safe environment. Interweaving her scholarship and four decades of activism, she has created both a ground-breaking theoretical framework for a new paradigm of personal and social change, and a powerful workshop methodology for its application. Her wide-ranging work addresses psychological and spiritual issues of the nuclear age, the cultivation of ecological awareness, and the fruitful resonance between Buddhist thought and contemporary science. The many dimensions of this work are explored in her books *Despair and Personal Power in the Nuclear Age* (New Society Publishers, 1983); *Dharma and Development* (Kumarian Press, 1985); *Thinking Like a Mountain* (with John Seed, Pat Fleming, and Arne Naess; New Society Publishers, 1988); *Mutual Causality in Buddhism and General Systems Theory* (SUNY Press, 1991); *World as Lover, World as Self* (Parallax Press, 1991); *Rilke's Book of Hours* (with Anita Barrows, Riverhead, 1996); and *Coming Back to Life: Practices to Reconnect Our Lives, Our World* (with Molly Young Brown, New Society Publishers, 1998). Joanna has also written a memoir entitled *Widening Circles* (New Society, 2000).

(From www.joannamacy.net)

Tim Merry

Tim Merry is a learner and expert in living systems, leadership, organisational change, business start-up consultancy, chaordic design (www.chaordic.com), community building, hosting and convening conversations that matter, community theatre, community music and the art of living a joyful life. He has spent years organizing, designing, and hosting inspired spaces – dialogues, strategic change processes, learning conferences, circle councils, networked organizations, communities of practice, coaching heroes in business – all in support of life-affirming leadership, collaborative learning, organizational and social change and self-organization.

"I believe we can create new ways of working, being and living if we just go for it. From our courage and passion now the organisational and community operating systems of the future will be born."

Tim currently lives in Nova Scotia, Canada, building up a learning centre on a beautiful piece of land in Yarmouth County (www.oftheshire.org). He is a student of meditation, loves playing/listening to music and writes and performs slam poetry and rap. His band, Kongska, is currently preparing an EP for release – check out some tunes at www.kongska.com.

George Pór

George's passion is to catalyse the collective consciousness, intelligence and effectiveness of communities of change champions working with or in organisations. He has been designing, hosting, and facilitating hundreds of virtual communities since 1982. He combines European values with American dynamism, ancient wisdom traditions and electronic technologies for collaboration and coordination.

He has held academic posts at the University of Lund in Sweden, the California Institute of Integral Studies, UC Berkeley, as Senior Research Fellow at INSEAD and Visiting Researcher in the Complexity Programme of the London School of Economics. He is currently PrimaVera Research Fellow in Collective Intelligence at Universiteit van Amsterdam Business School. He has authored "The Quest for Collective Intelligence", and "Liberating the Innovation Value of Communities of Practice".

George is the founder of CommunityIntelligence Ltd, an organisational transformation agency, and co-founder of the Evolutionary Leadership Action Network. He speaks English, French, Russian, Hungarian, and some Polish. He enjoys coaching and mentoring both visionary leaders and young professionals if they are equally committed to personal, organisational and social transformation. See:

http://www.communityintelligence.co.uk/who/george.htm
http://www.collectivewisdominitiative.org/files_people/
Por_–George.htm

Follow-up

To find out more about evolutionary leadership, I would recommend exploring the following key sites:

- www.evolutionary-leadership.com – latest links around the book

- www.petermerry.org - more about me, my work and life

- www.humanemergence.nl – putting it into practice in the Netherlands

- www.thehaguecenter.org – putting it into practice globally

- www.engagency.nl – putting into practice at work

- www.spiraldynamics.net – Spiral Dynamics Integral

- www.integralinstitute.org – the home of Ken Wilber's crew

- www.integralleadershipreview.com – online periodical with articles, interviews and reviews

- www.integral-review.org – online journal addressing integral theory, adult development. complexity theory

- www.enlightennext.org – Andrew Cohen's work

Integral Publishers

733 Mermaid Avenue
Pacific Grove, CA 93950
831 333-9200
http://www.integralleadershipreview.com
russ@integralleadershipreview.com

Integral Publishers was founded as the publishing house for the **Integral Leadership Review**. The Integral Leadership Review is the world's premier publication of integrated approaches to leadership. It serves leaders, professionals and academics engaged in the practice, development and theory of leadership.

We are the publishers of **LeadingDigest**. Each month we publish summaries of innovative material from the leading and groundbreaking ejournal, Integral Leadership Review. In the ejournal we publish extensive materials on leadership. In **LeadingDigest** we provide summaries that point directly at the key points of ILR material. Here you will find the key points and creative ideas of CEOs, as well as other practitioners, theorists and developers of leadership.

We also publish a series of books drawn from the pages of **Integral Leadership Review**:
    Insights on Leadership, Volume 1, Research and Theory
    Insights on Leadership, Volume 2, Developing Leaders
    Insights on Leadership, Volume 3, Executives
These volumes include interviews with top practitioners and thinkers about leading, leadership and its development.

Our books are by integrally informed authors on a variety of topics. Additional books forthcoming:

Jordan McLeod, **The New Currency**
Robert Rabbin, **A Mystic in Corporate America**
Yene Assegid, **Butterflies over Africa**